A Nation on Trial

France and the Legacy of the Dreyfus Affair

A Nation on Trial

France and the Legacy of the Dreyfus Affair

Margery Elfin

Washington, DC
2016

*I publish this for my grandchildren, as a reminder of
the power of history and the principle of justice.*

*I thank my husband, Mel Elfin, and my children, David and Dana,
for supporting my effort, along with my sister, Dee Garbose.*

*I am particularly grateful to Lee Cannon
for bringing this manuscript into coherent print form.*

Table of Contents

Chronology of the Dreyfus Affair

The context is France after a humiliating defeat in the Franco-Prussian War (1871).

Dreyfus, born in 1859 and raised in Alsace, is old enough to remember the war and at a very young age becomes very patriotic and wants to restore France's reputation. He attends military school.

Esterhazy, born in 1847, is at the time of the Affair a young lieutenant constantly in need of money. He is guilty of the crime with which Dreyfus is charged—selling secret military information to the Germans.

1894

Esterhazy offers to provide intelligence to the German Embassy and deals with Schwarzkoppen, the military attaché. Although France and Germany are not at war, Germany, as a newly unified military power, is anxious to know what the French level of preparedness is.

Information contained in a *bordereau* (brief memorandum) arrives at the embassy in September and is found in a waste basket by a cleaning woman who acts as an agent for the French high command. She delivers it to French intelligence. Dreyfus, as an Alsatian and a Jew, is accused of writing the *bordereau*. He is arrested in October.

The investigating officers, all anti-Semitic, spread word of treason, which is picked up by Paris newspapers. The military wishes to avoid charges of incompetence and are looking for a scapegoat. The case hinges on the dubious testimony of a handwriting expert. By December, a court martial is ordered and held in secret. Dreyfus had been kept incommunicado since his arrest. He is condemned to exile; an appeal on the last day of the year is denied.

1895

In January, Dreyfus is subject to a degradation ceremony in which he is publicly stripped of his military insignia and his sword is broken. The crowd shouts, "Death to the Jews!" He is imprisoned on the Île de Ré for a month before being transported to Devil's Island, where he will serve nearly five years in solitary confinement in the heat and dirt of the tropics.

1896

Lieutenant Colonel Picquart, new head of the Intelligence Service, finds another paper in the file, *le petit bleu*, and orders an investigation. By August, he is sure Esterhazy is the guilty party. The French military leadership refuse to consider his report, assign him overseas, and begin a coverup operation.

1897

Picquart protests from his post in North Africa and discusses the situation with a lawyer. At the same time, he writes an addendum into his will with the whole story.

The plot begins to unravel as the pressure steadily increases from Dreyfus' family and from Picquart's disclosures to the French Senate. Attention focuses on Esterhazy. An investigation is conducted, but handwriting experts continue to insist that he is innocent of writing the *bordereau*. The military refuses to prosecute.

Media coverage accelerates and the case, now known as "The Dreyfus Affair," polarizes French society.

1898

By January, the army, under pressure from a newly constituted Assembly and Senate, court-martials Esterhazy, but finds him innocent.

January 13—The acquittal of Esterhazy and the resulting anti-Semitic fervor compels Zola to write his famous letter, "J'Accuse," published first in *L'Aurore* and subsequently republished in other newspapers. Also, Picquart is arrested.

January 18—The Minister of War sues Zola and *L'Aurore* for libel.

January 24—The German government denies any relations with Dreyfus.

February 7—Zola is tried.

February 23—Zola is sentenced to a year in prison and fined 3,000 francs.

February 26— Lieutenant Colonel Picquart is dismissed from the army.

July 19—Zola flees to England.

July 23—Zola's name is stricken from the Legion of Honor.

August 13—Commandant (equivalent of a Major) Henry's forged documents are discovered. He is arrested and allegedly commits suicide in military prison. There is considerable doubt it was actually suicide and not simply another coverup by the army.

September 25—Esterhazy states publicly that he wrote the *bordereau*, but under orders from Colonel Sandherr.

November 24—Picquart court-martialed.

December 2—Picquart demands a change in venue.

1899

March—The Court of Cassation begins investigation into the secret dossier.

June 3—The Court sets aside the decision of 1894 condemning Dreyfus and refers the matter to a new court-martial at Rennes.

June 5—Zola returns to France.

June 9—Dreyfus leaves Guiana for France. Picquart is freed.

August—The second court-martial begins.

September 9—Dreyfus condemned once more, but not unanimously.

September 19—Dreyfus is pardoned.

1900

December 27—An Amnesty Bill is passed, stopping all suits arising out of the Dreyfus case.

1901

Dreyfus publishes his journal of his imprisonment, *Five Years of My Life*.

1902

September 30—Zola dies in a bizarre household accident.

1903

November 26—Dreyfus appeals for a revision.

December 24—The case is placed before the Court of Cassation. It drags through the French court system until July 12, 1906 when the Court sets aside the Rennes judgment and orders the "rehabilitation" of Dreyfus.

July 13—Dreyfus promoted to commandant; Picquart to brigadier-general.

July 20—Dreyfus is restored to the army in a ceremony at the École Militaire. He is made a Chevalier of the Legion of Honor.

1906

July 12—Dreyfus officially "rehabilitated."

1908

June 4—Zola's ashes transferred to the Pantheon. Dreyfus is wounded by an assailant during this ceremony.

1914

Picquart dies in a fall from a horse. Dreyfus returns to active duty in World War I and is promoted to Lieutenant Colonel.

1923

Esterhazy dies in London.

1935

Dreyfus dies in Paris.

Chief chronological source: Snyder, Louis L. *The Dreyfus Case: A Documentary History*. Rutgers University Press: New Brunswick, NJ, 1973.

Introduction
More Than Just a Trial

CRIMINAL TRIALS HAVE ALWAYS INTRIGUED the public imagination, and with good reason. There is an element of relief in our fascination (that could be me on the stand), a desire to see someone punished, along with simple voyeurism, that compelling curiosity about other peoples' motives and lives. In a way, following a trial permits us to view the worst aspects of human beings from a safe distance. We can identify without involvement. An emotional need is satisfied without risk.

Political trials, however, go beyond the personal and our human attraction to the frailty and imperfection in our peers, for they are not merely about the fate of one person. They are worth examining because they often represent powerful social trends, which can be cataclysmic in their capacity to shape the thinking of future generations. It is these trials that capture our imaginations and help us understand both history and the times in which we live. They are tests of values and, accordingly, they have a universal appeal.

When individuals on trial have served as symbols of political and social conflict, they have often been unwitting (and unwilling) servants of ideologies. Their trials reached well beyond their individual cases to reflect the complicated social and political forces that brought them to the courtroom.

History has been the final judge of their importance. When we look back at Sacco and Vanzetti from our vantage point, for example, we probably see two pathetic anarchists caught in a judicial process they did not understand and it is hard to imagine the fears that these two Italian immigrants aroused in many Americans. Anarchism is certainly not an issue today. On the other hand, the teaching of creationism, which resulted in such an outpouring of religious fervor in the 1920s, remains a matter of concern in many states and is still hotly debated in educational circles. What is going on, or not going on in society, that settles one issue decisively and not another?

Some of the people accused in the cases that interest students of political trials were supporters of unpopular beliefs—like John Scopes, who taught evolution as part of his high school biology course in Tennessee, or Sacco and Vanzetti, the Italian anarchists thrust into a confusing and hostile political system. Others, like the Scottsboro Boys, unfortunately served by happenstance as surrogates for the racial hatred and prejudices of their time. Some actively sought the limelight to publicize their cause, like Susan B. Anthony, the great feminist arrested for voting in Rochester, New York. Others, like the young Captain Dreyfus, were forcibly cast into the limelight and refused to believe their cases represented anything larger than an unintended miscarriage of justice.

When political trials are polarizing events, we learn a lot from the intense battles between conservatives and progressives over maintaining or changing the status quo. We analyze their outcomes, finding in them an explanation of winners and losers in the particular context in which the trials were held, as well as the long term effects of the battle, e.g. the weakened position of the Church and military in France, as in the Dreyfus case, or the deeply embedded fear of communism in the United States as in the trial of the Rosenbergs and other communist trials in the 1950s.

In many ways, modern political trials prove to be satisfying group experiences. They bring a sense of closure to divisive issues, at least in societies where judicial decisions are accepted as valid and binding. They afford an opportunity for those people who have taken positions to vent their feelings and for the less involved to inform themselves on the issues. Here, the media play an increasingly important role in keeping the issues in public view and thus raising consciousness for the general reader or viewer. They are open forums for important debates over values.

The Sixth Amendment of the U. S. Constitution guarantees the right to a speedy and public trial. For years, it was thought that although "speedy" was certainly open to interpretation, "public" seemed clear enough. Now with the advent of television and the Internet, the two most common means of obtaining news, the word "public" also requires redefinition so that we have a common standard by which to judge, for example, the controversy over allowing cameras in the courtroom and their relationship to the vague right of the public to "know." How much does publicity (derived from the public) determine the course and outcome of a trial? One of the memorable aspects of the second Dreyfus trial is that he was truly tried in the press—a first for our times. This generated considerable mistrust of the media and its role in manipulating the public. More than a century later, we are still debating the extent to which we can preserve freedom of the press and guarantee fairness in a trial.

On some levels political trials are show trials, public lessons in dispute resolution open to anyone who cares to listen. It goes without saying that this is important in a democratic society. The problem, of course, is the trustworthiness of the information received and the potential for manipulation in a media age. When trials are deliberate show trials, as were those orchestrated by the Soviets, they serve the purpose of the state. Even the Nuremberg trials fit the show trial model to the extent that it was important for democratic regimes to make a public statement about crimes against humanity by means of an orderly, legal process. Since political trials may threaten the stability of governmental institutions, they require this sort of official response if the government is to maintain power.

Although we do not today have as partisan a press as the historic trials referred to above, journalistic objectivity still remains a goal, not a given. What distinguishes recent modern trials from historic ones is the overwhelming amount of information disseminated and the homogeneity of the message usually derived from a few major news outlets. At their best the media can enlighten the public and act as predictors of social change. Media coverage stimulates consideration of issues that might otherwise have remained beneath the surface. Political scientists refer to this phenomenon as agenda-setting. Another aspect of this is the opportunity the media provide interest groups to express their points of view in letters to the editor and op-ed pieces, which serve to raise visibility and provoke discussion.

Connected to this escalation in the number of participants is the response in the creative arena, where writers and artists have taken inspiration from the trials. Émile Zola, of course, is a prime example with his rousing call to action, "J'Accuse," but there are many others who have reacted to the drama of these trials by producing serious literary works: "Inherit the Wind," by Jerome Lawrence and Robert E. Lee, a fictionalized version of the Scopes trial; Maxwell Anderson's poetic "Winterset" about the Sacco-Vanzetti case; and Arthur Koestler's chilling *Darkness At Noon*, which captures the horrors of the Soviet legal system. These writings endure long after the actual trials are over and leave an intellectual legacy for generations after.

By the time of the Dreyfus Affair, at the end of the 19th century, media coverage had crossed national boundaries and aroused intense reactions from other countries. Dreyfus' was the first trial to be covered by an international press corps. William James, the American psychologist and writer, taking the cure at a German spa in August 1899, wrote "...everyone at Bad Nauheim is reading *Le Figaro's* account of the Dreyfus trial every day." [1] This sounds very much like the incredible, unremitting attention paid to the O. J. Simpson trial in the United States in the '90s, which was reported on in detail by television and the global tabloid press.

The trial, and the Affair that ensued, had all the ingredients of an improbable melodrama. In the case of Dreyfus, there were two trials, nearly five years apart. The flames were fed by the media, who created what some have called "mass hysteria." Who wouldn't want to read about trials in which accusations of lying, forged evidence, allegations of conspiracy, a shooting of an attorney for the defense, a few suicides along the way, and impassioned commentary by leading French intellectuals were prominently featured? Politicians feared that the Affair threatened France's position among the world powers and could not wait for it to end.

Important questions about the value of the information and the nature of espionage in peacetime were submerged in the flood of character assassination, much of it anti-Semitic, that followed. Dreyfus' family, particularly his brother, Mathieu, scrambled to find legal representation and develop a defense. It was not until the court-martial proceedings had begun that Dreyfus was permitted to see a lawyer and to communicate with his wife. For two weeks he was subject to interrogations. The treatment of Dreyfus while he awaited his court-martial was horrendous and violated military standards.

The response of Theodore Roosevelt, then governor of New York, to the Affair, reflects his usual certitude. "It was less Dreyfus on trial than those who tried him. We should draw lessons from the trial. It was due in part to bitter religious prejudices of the French people."[2] There is a tone of self-satisfaction in this blunt acknowledgement of the cultural aspects of political trials and the perception of an astute American politician, who understood the need to accommodate an increasingly diverse ethnic constituency.

Writers have always found the outsider fighting the system a stimulating topic for their imaginations. An individual persecuted for dissent from a regime or a prevailing value system presents an inherently dramatic situation. The human tendency towards pack behavior and the corresponding proclivity for scapegoating are universal and timeless subjects. What does change is context. Think about the following questions. Would Scopes be convicted today? Would the Scottsboro boys have been sentenced thirty or forty years later? What about the Rosenbergs? Would they have gone to their deaths? It becomes apparent that it is not only the legal evidence of the trials that is determining, but the public response that affects the outcome.

The dissenters of the past often become the standard bearers of the future as values change over the years. How much are our ideas of justice affected by the politics of the time? These speculations are fertile ground for historians, philosophers, and writers. Not unexpectedly, the trials become more memorable and vivid as they penetrate the popular culture through literature and film or theater. The fictional characters often assume a greater reality than the living people.

The political trial is a barometer of social change, as is the conflict that accompanies it. The Dreyfus Affair is a particularly good example of this phenomenon, for it still resonates in the social divisions of contemporary France. Many of its underlying conflicts have not yet been resolved, despite well-intentioned efforts to create an image of a unified French culture. Although some of the arguments are presented in a civilized way, the clash of values remains an irritant. And contrary to belief, political decisions, as these judicial ones were, do not progress in straight lines, but show the dominance of certain values in specific time periods. In France, the ideologies of republicanism and anti-republicanism have cycled in and out through the last few centuries. This core disagreement over the direction in which France should go has been a source of deep social fissures many times during the more than one hundred years since a young army captain was falsely accused. Despite the passage of time, the Dreyfus case remains imprinted in the French culture, and in the minds of people all over the world who care about justice. It has left an enduring and disturbing legacy.

One

The Affair: The First Trial

From Accusation to Exile

Decidedly, military tribunals have a singular idea of justice.
—*Émile Zola*

THE DREYFUS AFFAIR sounds a discordant note in the popular image of turn-of-the-century Paris—a city of lights, filled with music, dance, and theater. A generation of painters and early photographers have transmitted shimmering visual images of the city that picture a life of pleasure and ease for the rich. For the poor, well, Zola has described in shattering detail the gritty lives of the overworked, underpaid, and unhealthy people who comprised the majority of a supposedly carefree society. But Zola was scorned and denigrated by French society as one who discomfited them with his criticism of their lifestyle. It is fitting, then, it was Zola, the chronicler of working-class France, who became intimately connected with the key event of his time—the Dreyfus Affair—and further eroded the complacency of the rich and well-born.

It seems improbable that one small piece of paper, discovered in a wastebasket in the German embassy in Paris with a few handwritten notes scrawled on it, could have cost a man his freedom and dominated French politics for twelve years. Yet that is what happened, to the discredit of France, when the French army framed a young Jewish officer for treason in 1894. Accusations of treason do not usually arise without serious investigation, yet the Dreyfus case stands as a glaring exception to the rule. Even more than a century later, the framing of accused persons in everyday criminal cases is unsurprising; police everywhere in both democratic and undemocratic societies are frequently guilty of this. But a question of treason, a political crime, is a different matter.

The carelessness of the proceedings against Dreyfus was shocking. For more than a century, historians, writers, and political scientists have examined the Dreyfus Affair in detail. No one believes there was sufficient evidence to bring suit and certainly not enough to convict Captain Alfred Dreyfus. However, military justice, as has been said with some truth, is to justice what military music is to music. Thus the Dreyfus case became the most celebrated cause of the 19th century. It had all the dramatic ingredients that accompany a blatant miscarriage of justice—the requisite villains, a persecuted hero, and an excited public spurred on by the hyperbolic excesses of the media.

The chief criticism of the case is that many of the standard procedural guarantees were not afforded the young captain. Military codes of justice, however, are not identical to the civil codes of a country. Later, when more of the facts became known, lawyers and writers in other countries would compare the French proceedings to those of their own. An English authority made such a comparison in the *Westminster Review* of January 1898.[1] He concluded that what happened to Dreyfus could never have happened in England. He criticizes the "profound secrecy" of the proceedings, the fact that the preliminary inquiry took 27 days, during which the prisoner was not informed of the charges nor was his lawyer permitted to view all the evidence. Furthermore, the Minister of War, General Mercier, granted an interview to a newspaper, *Le Figaro*, in which he condemned Dreyfus and proclaimed that his guilt was a certainty.

The author continues by saying the Ministry of War worked hand in glove with the media to give out the "official version." The English would not have tried a case of selling military secrets in peacetime as treason. This traffic in information was apparently not an unusual occurrence. Moreover, treason would have been tried by courts of common law. The accused would have been given the names of the officers who would try him, were it a standard court-martial, and he would have had the opportunity to communicate freely with legal advisers and witnesses. An English general would not have gone to the press with the case. Finally, the author calls the court-martial an example of "distorted ingenuity" and "prisoner-baiting." Hardly an instance of English "fair play."

The case against Dreyfus, hastily assembled, was full of holes and fabrications, bound to unravel in the light of day, but the army was willing to take the risk the truth would never come out. To an extent and for a long period of time, they were right. They held the advantage of secrecy. Despite the evidentiary flaws, Dreyfus endured nearly five years of solitary imprisonment—a situation that was truly Kafkaesque. Given its extremely harsh treatment of the prisoner, it is likely the army did not expect the case to resurface. Those who had so summarily prosecuted the hapless captain must certainly have thought the uncomfortable situation would be permanently relegated to oblivion. It would be just another forgotten miscarriage of justice in a long history of such travesties. They failed, however, to anticipate the devotion of Dreyfus' family, its ability and willingness to spend huge sums of money in his defense, a massive campaign in the newspapers, a blizzard of pamphlets, and the incendiary prose of a celebrity author, Émile Zola, which brought the case to public attention.

As we have noted, there was no evidence from the very beginning that would hold up in open court. Accordingly, from the military point of view, it was understandable that the proceedings were held in secret and the evidence kept from both the defendant and his lawyer. Rights which we now consider basic, such as the right of the accused to be present throughout an investigation, the right to confront witnesses, the right to examine evidence, the right to present additional evidence, and the right to remain silent, were not afforded Captain Dreyfus.

Dreyfus' nightmare began in the fall of 1894 when he was brought in for questioning by his superiors with no advance notice. Posted in Paris on assignment to the General Staff, he was enjoying the life of a well-to-do officer in a fashionable apartment with his family, usually walking to and from work and keeping regular hours. It was a career and lifestyle many would envy. His daily routine was the unexceptional one of a military man in a peacetime army, with the luck to be stationed in Paris.

One Saturday in October, he received a summons to appear in civilian dress at headquarters the following Monday morning, October 15. No information was given to him and no information was provided to his family. This, of course, runs counter to modern ideas of due process. He was detained at headquarters with no reason given. Lucie, his wife, ten years younger than he and the mother of their two young children, was terrified when Colonel du Paty de Clam, one of the instigators of the conspiracy against Dreyfus, arrived at their home to begin a search, warning her not to tell anyone of her husband's arrest. Nor would the army make the arrest public. He said only that Dreyfus was a spy—a statement so preposterous that Mrs. Dreyfus thought there had to be some egregious mistake. No one could have foreseen Dreyfus would not set foot in his home again for years. He remained for days confined in the Cherche-Midi prison in Paris with no communication to the world outside the prison gates. He had no idea what the charges against him were; it was a nightmare situation. So far, Dreyfus had been denied his rights each step of the way.

After his initial rage, when he frightened his jailer by hurling objects in his cell, Dreyfus lapsed into a state of shock and disbelief, pacing endlessly and frequently shouting his innocence. Imagine the horror of an overnight change from a comfortable, upper-middle-class life to a prison cell where no one was permitted to talk to him. He was forbidden from communicating with anyone beyond the prison walls, while his wife was under orders to keep the news of his imprisonment to herself for the time being. Dreyfus' situation is eerily reminiscent of the continuous "legal" interrogations of alleged communists described in Arthur Koestler's *Darkness at Noon*. Worse was to come.

The commandant of the prison, Commandant Ferdinand Forzinetti, sympathized with Dreyfus, but the military high command was adamant in pursuing the questioning of the weakened prisoner and was determined to obtain a confession that he had committed treason. Dreyfus continually begged to see the document he had heard incriminated him. He was subjected to innumerable mysterious tests of his handwriting without comment. The prisoner demanded to see his wife and children, alternately crying and laughing in a hysterical state until the director of the prison feared he would lose his mind and appealed to the authorities for help, to no avail.

It seems what was underway in this peculiar handling of the prisoner was a campaign directed against Dreyfus in order to maintain the honor of the military. The allegations, soon to harden into specific charges, were that a document of French military intelligence had found its way into the German embassy in Paris. This document, known as a *bordereau*, was a memorandum describing artillery weapons and outlining reorganization plans for mobilization. The information contained was material to which Dreyfus was not privy. It was two weeks before Dreyfus would be shown this "proof" of his treason. All the samples of handwriting had been taken to establish that Dreyfus had written the *bordereau*. The mystery of how it was found in a wastebasket at the German embassy by a cleaning woman was not yet revealed, although it was later established that the woman was herself an agent for the French intelligence service, such as it was. The accusation of treason hinged on the opinion of one man, Alphonse Bertillon, a handwriting expert in the pay of the military.

By the time Dreyfus was court-martialed in December, he had been held for six weeks in execrable conditions. The High Command had launched a slanderous attack on him in military circles and in the anti-Semitic popular press, painting him as a womanizer and a gambler. Some of the accusers, like du Paty de Clam, were obsessively anti-Semitic. He had hastily assembled a huge dossier on every aspect of Dreyfus' private life; it was clear the army wanted to settle its spy problem by defaming the character of Dreyfus. In this effort, they had the eager assistance of Commandant Hubert-Joseph Henry, an officer so anxious to please his superiors that he was capable of falsifying documents and evidence.

Important questions about the value of the information and the nature of espionage in peacetime were submerged in the flood of character assassination, much of it anti-Semitic, that followed. Dreyfus' family, particularly his brother, Mathieu, scrambled to find legal representation and develop a defense. It was not until the court-martial proceedings had begun that Dreyfus was permitted to see a lawyer and communicate with his wife. For two weeks, he was subjected to more interrogations. The treatment of Dreyfus while he awaited his court-martial was horrendous and violated military codes of conduct, but his family was powerless. All of his family's requests to see him were denied and he was not provided with any of the amenities due an officer who, after all, had yet to be found guilty or innocent.

Finally, on December 19, the case was scheduled to be heard. By this time, so many high level reputations hung on his conviction that an acquittal would have meant certain disgrace for his superiors. Dreyfus "had" to be guilty for the sake of the army's reputation. Thus began an intensive cover-up and tampering with files to assure a guilty verdict. Officers in the so-called Section of Statistics, whose intelligence files provided the basis of the accusation, undertook extensive editing of documents. This chicanery was unknown to Dreyfus' lawyer, who, in effect, was forced to operate in the dark, relying on the minimal information provided by the High Command.

Over the defense's objections, the proceedings took place in closed session. The rationale for this was the danger of a breach of security. Behind-the-scenes maneuvering by the prosecution resulted in Commandant Henry, who engineered most of the fabrications, making a theatrical appearance before the judges, in which he swore to the treasonous behavior of Dreyfus and gestured theatrically to a painting of Christ on the wall to make his point. It was hard to miss the crude anti-Semitic allusion. Henry was one of those officers who disapproved of Jews in the ranks. His open anti-Semitism was so typical of the times, though, his dramatic courtroom gesture was not perceived or mentioned as remarkable.

It was later learned that, in the course of the judicial deliberations, a sealed envelope with a number of documents enclosed had been opened and passed around to be read by the panel. The defense never saw this information, although there was enough of it to extend the deliberations for hours. Finally, the judges arrived at a unanimous decision: Dreyfus would be deported and imprisoned for life. Furthermore, he would be subject to degradation, a public event in which he would be stripped of his military insignia and disgraced before his peers.

Why didn't Dreyfus' superiors let the matter rest? After all, no one ever needed to know the *bordereau* had been discovered. Why was it so important to see such a shaky case through? These are, of course, questions raised in hindsight. Perhaps the military was still experiencing the humiliation suffered at the hands of the Germans in the Franco-Prussian war and were ready to believe that Germany was still plotting against France. It seemed natural that an Alsatian should help the German cause. Many of the officers simply accepted as fact that Dreyfus was a traitor, giving credence to the handwriting analysis and the propaganda distributed by the General Staff. Admittedly, there was fertile ground here, because of the inherent predisposition to anti-Semitism. More importantly, there was a desire to believe no true French officer would betray his country, so it was a relief to discover that it was a Jewish officer and an Alsatian who was guilty.

Reaction to the sentence demonstrated how little support Dreyfus had, both within the army and with the public. Those who spoke out in the press complained the sentence was too lenient. Many asked for the return of the death penalty for treason, which had been abolished in the Constitution of 1848. One of those who did was the socialist Jean Jaurès. At this point, he was entirely unsympathetic to Dreyfus' plight. In fact, no one on the right or the left seemed willing to side with Dreyfus. Not only did they believe him to be guilty, but they were out for blood. The army had found a traitor and punished him. The matter appeared to be clearcut; there was a widespread feeling of relief.

It is interesting to compare reactions in 1895 with those in 1899 when Dreyfus was brought back from solitary confinement on Devil's Island to be retried in Rennes. By then, the press was no longer united in opposition to Dreyfus. There had been a significant change in public opinion since four years before, when most of the public believed Dreyfus was guilty. The many factors at work in turning the tide for Dreyfus will be discussed in Chapter Seven, in an examination of the media's role.

The degradation ceremony was the first indicator public furor encouraged by the military would overtake logic and the course of justice. One example of the determination to humiliate a Jew was the choice of Saturday, the Jewish sabbath, as the day for the degradation ceremony, in which Dreyfus would be stripped of his military insignia and his sword would be broken. Eye-witness descriptions of this ceremony abound and all are graphic and moving. A proud young officer, body rigid, head erect, is marched out in the courtyard of the École Militaire. The public, alerted by the press, crowded the gates trying to get in, much like excited onlookers at a hanging. It was a ceremonial occasion, with uniformed men on horseback escorting Dreyfus in a coach from prison. There were military units in full dress standing at attention to the sound of ominous drum rolls as the prisoner stood before General Paul Darras and his peers, awaiting his humiliation. A reporter for the *New York Herald*, who witnessed the ceremony on January 5, 1895, described the emotion and excitement of the scene:

> The degradation of Dreyfus caused a profound excitement among the Parisian public. Not less than twenty thousand persons, who were kept at a distance from the scene surrounded the square and hooted at the prisoner throughout the ceremony, shouting: "Death to the traitor! Death to the Jews! [2]

It was a spectacle that drastically changed the direction of one observer's life. Theodor Herzl, a reporter for a Viennese newspaper who was later to become the spearhead of political zionism and the inspiration for the creation of the state of Israel, was assigned to cover the ceremony. Herzl, an assimilated Jew with no religious background worth mentioning, was horrified to hear in the angry shouts of the crowd, "*A mort les Juifs!*" He could not believe that in France, a country regarded as a model of republican government unique on a continent of monarchies and repressive regimes, such an assault on the civil liberties of a Jewish officer could take place. He later said on that day he became a Zionist. For if this expression of unchecked hatred could occur in republican France, where could Jews be safe? In response to this frightening thought, Herzl decided at that moment to dedicate his life to establishing a homeland for the Jews.

As for the Jewish community in Paris, there was little public comment. Many Jews feared for their own security and were reluctant to play any part in what might be a singular case. Others were convinced that Dreyfus was guilty and the wisest course was to lie low until the storm passed. They feared showing any sympathy for a traitor. After all, there were Jewish officers in the army and Jews were prominent in many of the professions and the arts, as well as politics. There were no ghettos as in other European countries. As far as they were concerned, France was a secular republic and a good place to live. As long as the Jewish community was orderly and quiet, Jews did not experience interference from the government and they were grateful.

When Dreyfus was virtually smuggled out of Paris in tight security on his way to the Île de Ré, off the west coast of France at La Rochelle, and then placed aboard a ship to Devil's Island, some breathed a sigh of relief. The Affair was over; the prisoner would begin his life sentence thousands of miles from France and away from the public eye. Those who believed that would be proved terribly wrong. The duration of the Affair was beyond anyone's imagination. It lasted twelve years, during which it permeated most aspects of French politics and culture. It would dominate the political sphere and literary circles—the salons that were the lifeblood of Parisian society. The intelligentsia quite literally dined out on Dreyfus. Even those who were disinterested in politics were drawn to the case for its human qualities. Before it came to a conclusion in 1906, it would polarize opinion and create deep enmities. It would radically change and wreck many lives.

Dreyfus, now far removed from his country and in solitary confinement, was powerless; he had no control over his destiny. The case was taken up by others, chiefly by his brother, Mathieu, who orchestrated the strategy to appeal for a retrial. The ocean voyage did not bode well for a happy ending to the prisoner's troubles. He was kept chained in a cage on deck for the first days of his journey and was treated as an ordinary criminal. Dreyfus had hoped that his family would be able to join him in exile, but this hope had proved futile. Lucie even spoke of leaving the children, whose health would be a major concern on Devil's Island, and accompanying her husband in exile. This plea was refused.

There were constant rumors in the press of a conspiracy to help Dreyfus escape (later determined to have been leaked by the anti-Dreyfusards)—an incredible story in light of the number of guards surrounding him and the remoteness of his location. His family lodged protests over his treatment, which were ignored. He suffered all the predictable maladies of exposure to the tropics, but his mental suffering exceeded the fevers and intestinal disturbances that plagued him constantly.

Yet despite the distance and the resulting slowness of communication, his family and a few friends doggedly pursued the case until it gradually evolved into a cause, attracting solid backing from people unknown to them. Although the Third Republic leadership thought they were rid of a potential embarrassment, the Affair was rapidly becoming a case that could not be ignored. Dreyfus, because his mail was censored, knew nothing of the campaign launched on his behalf and of course, he was not personally acquainted with those ardent supporters who were working to free him. He spent his days in his dark hut, writing his diary, studying English, reading Shakespeare (one of his major consolations) and keeping his mind sharp by solving difficult mathematical problems.

One of the most vocal advocates of the Dreyfus cause was Bernard Lazare, a Jew and something of a literary star in French intellectual circles because of a scholarly essay on anti-Semitism he had published in 1894, the year Dreyfus was accused of treason. He was not an observant Jew and believed that as Jews became more assimilated into French society, anti-Semitism would fade. For Lazare, like Herzl, the Affair was the catalyst that changed his thinking about the value of assimilation. Although, as a socialist, he had initially found nothing to merit his attention in the case of a well-to-do Jewish officer, at Mathieu Dreyfus' request, he agreed to become involved.

Politics and journalism intersected in the person of Bernard Lazare. He proved to be an indefatigable crusader for the Dreyfusards, so much so that he himself soon became the easily recognizable subject of the unflattering cartoons that appeared in quantity in the popular press. At the beginning of the case, the press was violently anti-Semitic, spearheaded by Édouard Drumont's *La Libre Parole*, a paper that took a staunch Catholic position that the Jews were an evil and dangerous group in French society, responsible for the financial troubles of thousands of small investors. As early as November 1, 1894, when the military leaked the story of Dreyfus' arrest, *La Libre Parole* ran a page-one story with this headline: "High Treason. Arrest of the Jewish Officer A. Dreyfus."

The casual use of the adjective "Jewish" is telling. Throughout the many years of the Affair, Jewish would always serve as the identifying adjective, appearing so often as a modifier of "traitor" that it became an accepted description of the accused. Many other Catholic papers followed Drumont's lead enthusiastically. By the time of the court-martial in late December, public opinion had been well-prepared to believe the army's point of view. Drumont's success in framing the issue is reflected in a quote from an anonymous columnist in his paper, "We have nevertheless a consolation; it was not a true Frenchman who committed the crime."[3] For a supposedly secular country, the power and reach of the Catholic papers was truly astounding.

A journalistic battle ensued between the extremists on the right, led by Drumont, and Lazare and Zola, who regularly excoriated the blatant anti-Semitism of their publications. The language and illustrations were brutal. The anti-Dreyfusards also had a base of support in parliament, where speeches decrying the role of Jews in the French economy were routine. It took Zola's famous polemic years later to change the perceptions engendered by the biased press coverage of the first court-martial.

Zola's celebrity made a tremendous impact. Newspaper readers could not fail to see the shift in the stories that appeared as more information became available and the image of Dreyfus as victim, published over and over again, gradually began to penetrate the public consciousness.

Lazare tried to convince sympathetic members of parliament and Jews to speak out, but in the early stages of the Affair, people were either indifferent or intimidated. Most Jews were frightened of retaliation against their businesses and families, making stories of a Jewish conspiracy ridiculous. Politicians who would later support Dreyfus were not yet ready to do so. For many, it was still not clear that Dreyfus was innocent. They did not feel the time was ripe for a spirited defense. Finally, the bitter battle of words metamorphosed into an actual duel between Lazare and Drumont, in which no one was hurt.

The anti-Dreyfusards spread the story that it was money that kept the Dreyfus campaign alive, that had he been an ordinary officer and not a Jew of means, the case would have died when he was exiled. This story did have some merit, because it took substantial resources to finance the investigation to exonerate Dreyfus that a poorer man could not have afforded. There were undoubtedly other cases of injustice that never attracted any attention. It was, however, the indefatigable work of his brother and the persistence of his wife that kept the case alive. Little by little, the patient efforts of Mathieu Dreyfus began to offer some hope. Giving up his own business interests to save his brother, he persevered in assembling pieces of evidence that demonstrated his brother's innocence and pointed to a conspiracy within the military. He became the nerve center of a network of those who came to be known as Dreyfusards.

Perhaps most significant in reinvigorating the Affair was the appointment of a new man to head French military intelligence. He was Lieutenant Colonel Georges Picquart, a respected officer, who had taught at the École de Guerre and whose integrity was unquestioned. He replaced the ailing Colonel Sandherr, who had permitted the machinations of Commandant Henry in manufacturing the case against Dreyfus. Although Picquart was an avowed anti-Semite, it was he who soon realized his duty was to unravel and expose the coverup, which, like all attempts to hide the truth, was ultimately bound to fail. This coverup far outstripped the original offense and became the focus of the Dreyfusards' efforts to expose the truth, as the military authorities attempted to hide it. With Picquart in charge, the case took on a new intensity and soon his superiors became exceedingly nervous about their ability to control his investigation. They found themselves in an embarrassing position, in imminent danger of exposure. Suddenly, there was considerably more at stake than the justice of the sentence of one man for treason.

Two

The Affair: The Second Trial
From Exile to Pardon

"...there must be an understanding between military and civil society on the very ground of law and justice."
—*Georges Clemenceau*

THE DREYFUS CASE MOVED INTO ANOTHER PHASE in 1896 when the army appointed Lieutenant Colonel Georges Picquart to head the Dreyfus investigation. Before long, the military would regret the choice, as they could see that the legal case was quickly evolving into a political affair. Picquart's suspicions were soon aroused and began to center on the man who would prove to be the true culprit, a commandant named Ferdinand Walsin-Esterhazy. He was a well-known man about town in Paris society, of dubious character, who was constantly in debt because of his dissipated lifestyle. Picquart's predecessor had told him to rely on his deputy, Commandant Henry, who had been on the case since the beginning, if he had any questions about the Affair. Since Picquart had no reason to doubt Dreyfus' guilt, he at first placed all his trust in Henry's "findings." It did not take long before he was to be disabused of his trust in his deputy.

The details of Henry's forgeries and fabrications are less important than the mindset of his superiors on the General Staff, who were content to have him take the initiative in building a case against Dreyfus. This readiness to accept whatever Henry provided fit the military culture of resisting criticism and standing together against "outsiders" who questioned the system. Content with what Henry produced, his superiors had demonstrated no curiosity about his methods. They liked Henry's conclusions because they fit the case they had made. Their interest in justice trailed far behind their first priority of not embarrassing the army.

It was the famous *petit bleu* that triggered Picquart's suspicions. This was a piece of paper found at the German embassy, much as the incriminating *bordereau* had been; it clearly pointed to Esterhazy as a spy. It consisted of fragments of a telegram on blue paper which had been carefully ripped up and carelessly thrown into a wastebasket, from which Madame Bastian, the French "agent cum charwoman," had retrieved it. So it was a coincidental discovery in Henry's absence on leave that put Picquart on to Esterhazy. The documents brought in by this "faux cleaning lady" at the German Embassy, who was in fact a member of French intelligence (she had been collecting scraps of discarded paper from the wastebaskets of the embassy for years, mostly love letters and inconsequential notes), changed his view of the case. Henry, who was the usual recipient of this second hand "intelligence," had not had time to go through the documents obtained and left it to his subordinate, who reconstructed the fragments of the blue paper memorandum.

The details, which seem to be straight out of a French farce, are too complicated to summarize here, but it is enough to say that the *petit bleu* indicated treason and was addressed to Esterhazy. However, it had never been sent; there was no stamp on it. Picquart also recognized the signature "C" as one that Schwarzkoppen, the German military attaché, often used. However, the French officers, again backing off from a more objective view of the situation, refused to pursue this line of investigation. Picquart was startled to see Esterhazy's handwriting on other documents delivered to the German embassy. He was now convinced that there was a link between the discovery of this memo and the *bordereau*, and quite possibly a frame-up to incriminate Dreyfus.

When Picquart persisted with his research into the matter, his superiors became increasingly agitated. It would be many years before the whole truth was acknowledged. For the moment it was enough to expose the treachery of Esterhazy, an officer in constant need of money. It was not unusual for officers to have a number of gambling debts, but Esterhazy's financial situation was desperate. The officers on the General Staff had tried to spread a story that Dreyfus was a womanizer and a gambler, but it was difficult to convince even the most biased observers of this. That the army would continue to back Esterhazy and condemn Dreyfus is hard to understand on the basis of the evidence. Years later, Schwarzkoppen would write in his diary that "Dreyfus had been condemned in Esterhazy's place,"[1] but by the time he admitted it, the case was long over. His superiors, like the French generals, maintained their distance from the developing case. Silence reigned among the military on the many inconsistencies in the evidence. It was a misguided effort to save the reputation of the army; there was no other explanation that made sense.

Picquart, caught up in the intricacies of his inquiry, did not report his discoveries to the General Staff immediately. Finally, when he confronted them with his proof, they were angered. Nevertheless, he continued his probe, hoping to establish the truth definitively. His superiors had cautioned him that the two instances of espionage, the original *bordereau* and the *petit bleu* incriminating Esterhazy, were separate and he was ordered not to attempt to tie them together. To be sure he would be out of their way, his commanding officers arranged for his transfer out of Paris, and out of his job.

Meanwhile, Henry used Picquart's absence as an opportunity to continue his forgeries and deceptions, intercepting documents sent to Picquart and altering them to show Picquart was in league with the Dreyfusards. He then forwarded these documents to the Ministry of Defense. Soon Picquart was posted to North Africa, where there were uprisings against France as a colonial power. Far removed from the scene and worried about his military career, Picquart told the whole story of the concocted case to his lawyer, so that whatever happened, someone would have the proof of the fabrication and the coverup.

Initially, Picquart had had no sympathy for Dreyfus; he had witnessed the degradation ceremony dispassionately, convinced of the man's guilt. Although he was no friend of the Jews, (as noted, he was an admitted anti-Semite), he believed in the code of honor of an officer and felt it was his duty to discredit a case that rested on untruths. He was to make an unlikely ally of Dreyfus' brother, Mathieu, in his quest for what the French called "revision" or reopening the case. This obligation he took upon himself nearly destroyed his military career when the High Command realized that Picquart could bring down the army with his accusations. Not only did the army have no case, it had manufactured one against Dreyfus. One commentator put it succinctly, "If Dreyfus were innocent, then France was guilty." And if this were so, then France might indeed be torn apart by opposing social forces because so much was at stake. This was the crux of the matter.

By 1897, the case seemed to be turning around, as many notable citizens began to express their skepticism in public. One of these was

Georges Clemenceau, a particularly enthusiastic advocate for revision of the Dreyfus case and well-placed to be influential in the matter. He had initially believed in Dreyfus' guilt. Now the political editor of *L'Aurore*, he wrote a huge number of columns asking for a review of the case. In fact, Clemenceau originated the title, "J'Accuse," for Zola's incendiary indictment of the French military and judicial system that appeared in *L'Aurore*. Zola may have been the spark that lit the flames for the Affair, but Clemenceau was surely the keeper of those flames, relentless in his almost daily columns in support of Dreyfus.

Some say his reasons were personal, because his own career had suffered as a result of falsified documents produced against him in the Panama Canal scandal. Bredin reports this in detail in his authoritative book, *The Affair*.[2] Whatever his primary motivation, Clemenceau's feeling of injustice was close to the surface and he joined the ranks of Dreyfusards along with Jaurès, the socialist leader who had originally opposed Dreyfus. Both would be strong advocates for a reconsideration of the case.

With the cast of characters rapidly expanding and the falsifications by Commandant Henry mounting, the outline of the Affair became very difficult to follow. Basic questions—such as what information was actually exchanged, who received it, and how it endangered French security in peacetime—were finally being asked in the salons of Paris, where the Affair was the principal subject of conversation. These habitués of the salons of a century ago were much like the observers of twentieth-century Washington scandals, who dined out on Nixon's Watergate fiasco and who assiduously followed Clinton's notorious dalliances with women and complicated financial maneuverings. It took a detail-oriented mind and/or an obsessive interest in the case to keep track of events. The media were happy to keep the pot boiling with provocative columns and cartoons. Dreyfus was definitely the topic of the day across all strata of French society.

Eighteen ninety-eight was a key year for the Affair. Captain Dreyfus had already spent three years on Devil's Island. The army was under intense pressure from a newly elected assembly and senate to move ahead and lay the rumors of its fabricated evidence to rest. Mathieu Dreyfus had denounced Esterhazy in the press so frequently that his name was now well-known. His superiors ordered a court-martial and then, in an incredible verdict, found him innocent in a matter of minutes (variously reported as three or four) which few could take seriously. Rather than settling the Affair, the acquittal earned more support for the Dreyfusards, while the anti-Semites celebrated.

Adding to the furor and attracting world attention was Émile Zola's publication of "J'Accuse" in January. Following this polemic, he went on trial in February for libel against the Minister of War, was sentenced to a year in prison, and was fined 3,000 francs. Esterhazy's acquittal had been the final straw in Zola's barely contained anger against the process that had condemned Dreyfus and he sought to force the army to confront its actions in the Affair. Zola had achieved his goal through his own well publicized trial; he had captured the attention of the world.

Barbara Tuchman describes the passions of the people who crowded the galleries at the trial which dominated the daily newspapers. Marcel Proust was a regular among them.[3]

On February 25, 1898, *The New York Times* editorialized:

> In France...there are no rules of evidence...Witnesses have appeared before the judges and have spoken their minds freely...They have repeated conversations that they have heard at second or third hand. All this is called testimony in France.[4]

In July, Zola fled France rather than go to prison and was welcomed as a hero in England by a small circle of supporters (he remained there for nearly a year, mostly incognito). By the end of the month, the High

Command, worried about his insistence on seeing the Dreyfus case through by a determined consideration of all the evidence, dismissed Picquart from the army. The charge against him was revealing information from secret files.

By far, the most alarming event of this turbulent year was the suicide of Henry—who had just been promoted for his loyalty and good work from commandant to lieutenant colonel in November 1897—in his jail cell. It was Esterhazy who said the General Staff had been behind the forgeries and who produced evidence incriminating both du Paty and Henry. For once, he was telling the truth. As usual, Henry lied under interrogation, but finally admitted that what he had done, he had done for his country. This pitiful character, the only man from an ordinary background who had come up through the ranks, was desperately trying to prove himself to his superiors by giving them the information they wanted, even though he had to invent it. The conspirators had used him for their own purposes and he had acquiesced in this.

Soon after he was taken to prison to await trial for forgery, he supposedly slit his throat. There is still doubt about whether the army had him killed to keep him quiet or whether he died by his own hand. Most sources report that the razor with which he allegedly slit his throat was closed when they found his body. Others said he was left-handed and could not have possibly made the wound. Henry's death rallied the most fervent anti-Dreyfusards into a frenzy of public activity in which they depicted him as a victim of all kinds of Jewish and masonic conspiracies and sought martyrdom for him as a patriot.

It was clear that no matter how sluggish the bureaucracy, both military and governmental, the facts would eventually be made public. The media, given its strong ideological orientation and class readerships, profited from keeping the story before the public. One compelling literary work helped them in this task. There is general agreement that the most important factor in forcing the military's hand was the rhetoric of Émile Zola's eloquent plea for justice. (This will be considered in Chapter Seven in a discussion of the role of the media).

As Dreyfus languished in his fourth year on Devil's Island, knowing nothing about the events in France, the wheels were slowly turning to win him a rehearing. The timing finally seemed right. Public interest was high and people were pressing for more information. Dreyfus' second court-martial would take place four-and-a-half years after his deportation, in a setting quite different from the first. The city of Rennes was the chosen location. It was thought that, in comparison with Paris, it would be a peaceful choice. With the press from many countries there and the world watching, this seemed unlikely; indeed the city soon was bursting at the seams. What was important to the defense was the opportunity to have the judicial process played out in the open, in contrast to the *in-camera* proceedings of the first court-martial. There could be no outrageous violation of the defendant's rights in this setting. Or could there?

Would the new evidence of a coverup change anyone's mind? Would the simple fact that the defendant had not received a fair trial because documents had been kept from his lawyer weigh in his favor? After the fact, those familiar with the French system of justice say the case should have been thrown out on procedural grounds, since it was built on fraudulent documents unknown to the defense. The investigation into Dreyfus' alleged espionage had been secret. No one, including the defendant, knew what his criminal acts had been and the court-martial was held out of public view with no press coverage. Tainted evidence, perjured testimony, and a flawed investigation in which no other suspects were considered should have been enough to free Dreyfus. How could the seven military judges have thought otherwise?

Nearly five years after Dreyfus' first court martial, another military court would consider whether the case merited revision. The second trial was held in late summer of 1899, from August 7 to September 9, only months before the Paris Exposition of 1900, an event the French were hoping would restore their national glory tarnished in the Franco-Prussian war. The trial quickly turned into a public spectacle, attracting huge press coverage and forcing the French to confront a problem they thought was safely relegated to the past. Attending the trial in Rennes became a social activity for fashionable people and they flocked to the small Breton city. This time, the drama would be a satisfying public display and the defendant—gaunt and ill, exhibiting all the signs of weakness and disorientation after his years of confinement—would be present for all to see.

The army could not alter one disturbing reality. Dreyfus' condition, physical and mental, was beyond disguise. He was a wreck, a horror to look at after so many years of solitary confinement, malnutrition, and illness. The nightmare of his captivity ignited the imagination of the public. His peculiar voice, reportedly monotone to begin with and now cracked from disuse, his haggard appearance, his unemotional demeanor were eerie, almost frightening. How would the army deal with the unmistakable evidence of the effects of their treatment of him?

One would have thought the open nature of this trial would force the army to reconsider its strategy and confront the truth of its mistake. Admitting a mistake, they could then acquit Dreyfus, acknowledge their error, and life could continue. But the army refused to make this choice and spare the country. Instead, they lined up their aging generals, led by Mercier, who had been Minister of War in 1894 and had turned his back to the truth then. They all took the stand as stubbornly convinced of Dreyfus' guilt as they had been five years previously, although they produced no new evidence. They persistently lied under oath, to the frustration of Dreyfus and his lawyers. General Mercier insisted that his belief in Dreyfus' guilt had even intensified over the years. This provoked a courtroom demonstration of hisses and boos, but when Mercier met the crowds outside, he was cheered. This exercise in self-deception on the part of the army, which would rather preserve the institution by supporting a known reprobate like Esterhazy than clearing an innocent man like Dreyfus, set up an impenetrable barrier to the truth.

Why did the army reject a change of heart the second time around? The issue had become so politicized, with a vast array of groups staking out positions, that they may have felt trapped. Once again they showed no concern for an individual wrongly accused, but sought only to maintain the reputation of an institution that might be further discredited, were there a not-guilty verdict.

Dreyfus' brother, who had spearheaded and coordinated the effort for a retrial, could not believe that seven loyal army officers would condemn his brother "based on a tattered paper of suspect origin of contested attribution." The facts, so carefully assembled, were of no importance. The anti-Semitic press went wild. The Dreyfusards responded. Clemenceau, who later published seven volumes of his almost daily columns on the Affair, offered an explanation, "The mind of the military castes will not allow force to be subject to reason." [5]

The momentum of the second trial could not be halted, however. It was a crisis for French society, pitting conservatives against the left, clergy and royalists against free-thinkers, chauvinists against cosmopolitans. The case had now become the Affair; it was no longer about a single instance of espionage by an army officer. As Ernest Lavisse, a contemporary observer said, "The Affair is to the trial what the sea is to a ship. It exceeds it infinitely." [6] The nation was awash with Dreyfus.

The boundaries had extended and blurred between the personal and the political. It was to be the trial of two centuries, since the outcome would determine the direction French politics took in the 20th century. The power of nationalism, along with the notion of Frenchness, were on trial along with Dreyfus. The importance of the Dreyfus Affair was further heightened as a global network of celebrity supporters became active in the campaign to exonerate Dreyfus.

The excitement in Rennes was palpable. There was heavy security, with troops on horseback lining the streets of a city filled with journalists and excited spectators. The defendant was not well, but reportedly was anxious to state his case and see justice done. Dressed in the uniform of an artillery officer, his hair prematurely gray, his body weakened, he could barely climb the stairs to take his seat in the courtroom. Was the trial really about this wasted man? The impression of debility was so great that some onlookers were not sure he would be able to comprehend what was happening.

Preparation for the trial was complicated by two lawyers for the defense who were vastly different in age and temperament. The elder was Edgar Demange, who had been with Dreyfus in court in 1894 and the other was a younger, fiery man named Fernand Labori. Labori advocated a hard-hitting trial that would force the army's hand. Demange was more moderate in his approach, wanting to free his client more than he cared about attacking a corrupt institution. Adding to the drama was the shooting of Labori on the streets of Rennes as he walked to the trial one day. He was wounded in the back, but was able to be present for the rest of the proceedings. The potential assassin was never found.

It was Demange who made the final argument for Dreyfus; he was unbelievably long-winded and precise. It is hard for us to conceive of a courtroom summation that lasted five hours. The crux of his peroration was that any doubt in the minds of the judges should lead to acquittal. At the same time, he was deferential, referring to the officers who had testified to Dreyfus' guilt as very distinguished. He did not question the sincerity of their convictions.

This measured oration, however, fell on deaf ears, for the testimony of General Mercier had prepared the ground for a conviction. He was bolstered by Maurice Barrès, a journalist whom we would label a fascist today. He insisted that this was a struggle over the legitimate authority of the military against the word of an officer who might be a spy. Casting the case as a fight for the honor of the nation, he made the decision a very difficult one for the judges. As the unofficial spokesman for the anti-Dreyfusards, he emphasized the politics of the Affair and the damage France would suffer if Dreyfus were acquitted.

When the guilty verdict was handed down, Barrès offered his gratitude to the officers who had won a "victory" for the army (two officers of the seven had actually voted for acquittal). He spoke, moreover, of a victory over foreigners and those who had no understanding of what it meant to be French. He asked that Frenchmen love those who had punished Dreyfus through the use of "clear French reason." He referred to the "traitor Dreyfus" whose very existence threatened the French state because he represented the "enormous power of the Jewish nationality which "threatens" the French nation.[7] Barrès used the word *chambardement* to illustrate the nature of this threat. The first meaning is upheaval, but the second is getting rid of, a meaning which can be interpreted as ethnic cleansing. This time, Dreyfus was sentenced to 10 years of prison for betraying his country.

The prime minister, Pierre Waldeck-Rousseau, was furious with the judicial panel. The sentence, coming just months before the World's Fair of 1900, was not in France's best interests. His attitude, expressed in memoranda sent to the commander-in-chief before the verdict, augured a major split between government and army. The Marquis de Gallifet had warned the prime minister that the "government must not enter into combat against the entire army frozen in a posture of moral resistance." He emphasized the army's deep rooted prejudice against acquittal. When General de Gallifet issued a decree after the verdict congratulating the military court, Waldeck-Rousseau was further enraged. The first phrase of de Gallifet's decree was to become famous for its supreme inaccuracy—"The incident is over!" he proclaimed.

Waldeck-Rousseau immediately began negotiating an arrangement for a pardon. The greater world public was horrified at the verdict and it appeared that other nations might very well boycott the Fair. The suggestion of a pardon divided the Dreyfusards, some of whom were opposed to any agreement that looked like an admission of guilt. Dreyfus himself had to be convinced and was strongly influenced by his family, who were concerned that he could not survive another imprisonment. They begged him to concede and agree to the pardon. At last, Jean Jaurès, the socialist leader, composed a brief statement for Dreyfus in which he proclaimed his innocence and accepted the pardon. Picquart was one of those concerned who opposed the pardon and was angry that the Affair had lost out to politics. Labori, Dreyfus' second lawyer, was infuriated there had been what was in his estimation a sell-out.

Waldeck-Rousseau, in his desire to bring closure to the Affair, issued an amnesty to anyone who had been connected with it. No one would be prosecuted for any criminal acts or misdemeanors in any lawsuit. His priority was to end conflict and remove the Affair from the public mind. This, however, was not compatible with Dreyfus' wishes. He wanted the truth to come out. He was not ready to close debate. He stated publicly that he would continue to seek vindication of his honor, though his family had convinced him to accept the pardon. Zola agreed that the past could not be "amnestied."

The pardon and the accompanying amnesty destroyed the unity of those Dreyfusards who had worked together for years to obtain Dreyfus' freedom. Soon all the principals were accusing each other of agreeing to what amounted to an admission of guilt or sacrificing the national interest and republican values for the short-range goal of one man's freedom. The divisive issue of the Affair, in personal terms, centered on the fragility of Dreyfus' health, whereas his supporters had transformed him into a symbol of all that was wrong with French institutions. The positions taken on this issue lasted until the end of their lives. Labori, Dreyfus' lawyer, after meeting with him to explain his concerns that justice had not been done and the fight should continue, never spoke to him or his brother again. Picquart, as a military man, was also alienated and wondered why he had bothered entering the fray for such an equivocal outcome. He was disillusioned and felt betrayed in a matter of honor—always his guiding principle as an officer.

These strong emotions underline the truth that the Dreyfus case was a political trial, extending far beyond Dreyfus the man. Accordingly, the result was disappointing to those who believed the Army had been permitted to win, while the republican cause of civil rights was sacrificed. It reinforced the army's ability to command public matters. The army's strategy of encouraging the public to think that if Dreyfus "won," the proud institution of the military would lose, had succeeded—or backfired, depending on one's point of view.

Later speculation was that Dreyfus had been the victim of an intricate plot developed by the Secret Service to confound the Germans through giving them misleading information on French artillery capability. In an article in a special edition of *L'Histoire*, compiled for the Dreyfus centennial, Jean Doise speculates that the army may very well have engaged in a "complex machination" to confuse the Germans into thinking the French were planning to test a particular rapid-fire cannon, although they never did. He asks whether the Secret Service invented the Affair and Dreyfus paid the price.[8] In any event, the Third Republic was once more shown to be weak and incapable of controlling the military.

The political impairment of the leadership and the lack of party strength in the parliament played directly into the army's hands. They had flaunted the power of the civilian government and the rule of law. This disturbed Clemenceau, who later testifying at the trial of Zola said, "Soldiers have no *raison d'etre* except as defenders of the principles which civil society represents." It was certainly a minority view for a military man. Unlike in the United States, where the president is clearly designated by the Constitution to be Commander-in-Chief (as his first obligation), the French president had no such authority. The importance of civil control over the military in a democracy cannot be overstated. For the Third French Republic, depending on one's perspective, either the army was out of control or the government was ineffective. Neither was a conclusion that would satisfy the reigning authorities.

Three

Dreyfus
The Disappointing Hero

Would Dreyfus have been a Dreyfusard?
—Question often asked by students of the Affair

THE DREYFUS AFFAIR ATTRACTED A FOLLOWING of dedicated believers in justice, but Dreyfus himself remained aloof from the fervent rhetoric and determination of these people. What was there about Alfred Dreyfus that puzzled and alienated his supporters and made him an unlikely candidate for hero worship? If we look to his childhood, what do we find that might explain his lack of personal charm? Judging by his biographical data, there doesn't seem to be any Freudian explanation.

Born in Mulhouse, Alsace 11 years before the Franco-Prussian War, Dreyfus was the youngest child in a large and prosperous Jewish family. His upbringing in a privileged household was entirely French, except for the observance of important Jewish customs and holidays. His primary language and culture in this Germanic province was French. It is possible that, as an Alsatian and a Jew, he felt a particular need to prove himself as a patriot by choosing a military career. Or his interest in the military might have stemmed from a certain rigidity in his personality.

Alsace is an industrial region of eastern France, bordering Germany and Switzerland. At the time of Dreyfus' birth it was home to a substantial Jewish population. In 1798, the city of Mulhouse (then Mulhausen, a Swiss republic) had signed a treaty of union with France, hoping to boost its economy by reducing trade barriers. Its economy was based on textiles. Alfred's father owned a textile mill and was sufficiently well-off to educate his large family of seven children. Young Alfred was doted on by his older sisters and had the luxury of full-time schooling. Although Jews were never to feel safe anywhere in Europe, in this tiny area of Alsace where the Dreyfus family established their home, they enjoyed a relatively untroubled existence. The Jewish community was solidly established and relationships were mostly harmonious with the people with whom they lived and did business daily.

Almost a hundred years earlier, Dreyfus' great-grandfather had settled in Rixheim in the Rhine valley. The Jewish community there was never a ghetto, although there were periods they were threatened as a community with expulsion, depending on economic conditions and whatever was happening politically in Paris at the time. Michael Burns, in his book *Dreyfus, A Family Affair*,[1] details the rollercoaster situation for Jews in Rixheim over the years. At times they were scorned; at times they were tolerated and could go about their business without fear. In general, the Protestants and Jews were allied by class as factory owners and adopted a paternalistic attitude towards the mostly Catholic, German-speaking workers they employed.

Despite his youth, Dreyfus could not help but be aware of the religious and national differences in his environment. Catholic, Protestant, Jewish,

German, Swiss, French—these were the fault lines along which lives were precariously balanced. The Jewish and Protestant manufacturers tended to have different labor policies from the Catholics; managing labor conflicts was a major part of the life of a businessman. Many Catholic workers were immigrants from other parts of Alsace and Germany, so they shared a natural hostility toward the mill owners. Groups lived apart from each other in mutual distrust—divided by language, religion, and ethnicity. The industrialists did not support the regime of Napoleon III and voted against him in a referendum held in May 1870, although the working class, feeling exploited and encouraged by the local press, voted for him. The plebiscite exacerbated the already serious class divisions and the enmity of Catholics against Jews and Protestants.

Given his economic circumstances and the orientation of his family and his education, it is not surprising that Alfred Dreyfus felt intensely French. By the outbreak of the Franco-Prussian War, he was also vehemently anti-German. In his journal from Devil's Island,[2] Dreyfus writes that the war was his "first sorrow." It is certainly unusual for a child to have such a strong personal response to a historical event. For him, the Germans were the barbarians at the gates. As they had surrounded and destroyed sections of Strasbourg, it was felt they might do so to Mulhouse when they marched through on their way to the interior of France. Napoleon III had seriously misjudged German preparedness and the French army, poorly mobilized, suffered ruinous defeats in Alsace, culminating at Sedan.

In a matter of months, the war was effectively over and, under the peace agreement, Alsace was returned to the Germans, over the objections of the majority of the people. Recall the famous sentimental short story, "La Derniere Classe," in which the Alsatian school master regretfully teaches his last class in French. The loss of language was a shattering blow. The huge out-migration of Jews to France after defeat says something about where Jewish loyalties (and interests) lay. Many, including Dreyfus' brother, Jacques, had fought on the French side. In 1872, Dreyfus' father had moved his family to Basel in Switzerland, but he wanted his two younger sons to have a French education and the next year sent them both to Paris. Mathieu and Alfred moved back and forth so much between Switzerland and different French locales (their older sister, Henriette had married and was living in Carpentras,) that they may well have felt like part of the vast stream of refugees seeking permanent residence. It is probable that the Dreyfus family would feel forever displaced.

Some of the preparatory schools the boys attended followed the British model—tough curricula and rigid discipline. This, of course, was not uncommon for children of the wealthy, but can this early experience have created the *froideur* of which so many of Dreyfus' potential admirers complained? Or was it simply the premature separation from his family and his familiar home? Psycholanalysis retroactively applied is not a very reliable means of judging influences on personality, but we do know that with a near identical background, his brother Mathieu did not evince any of the coldness and formality of his younger brother. We can only speculate on the relative influence of personality versus circumstance, nature versus nurture.

Dreyfus was a good student at the École Polytechnique, which would prepare him for the army. He did well in the math and engineering courses, but his special love was equitation. Riding was the high point of his years at the school. Yet he chose not the cavalry, but the artillery as his specialty when he graduated in 1880, 10 years after the Franco-Prussian War. He began his career imbued with a sense of discipline and loyalty. Since the army was not a usual career choice for a Jew, it would soon present difficulties for his advancement, particularly since he was too formal a person to relax and participate in the camraderie of an organization which depended on informal networks for success. He did not have the necessary political skills to put himself forward in an unwelcoming environment.

As a typical young officer with the cushion of an independent income, Dreyfus led a life of ease, enjoying the pleasures of Paris. Later, his casual liaisons with women of a certain type would be used against him in his trial. As noted in the first chapter, his superiors attempted to explain his alleged treason as a result of his need for money to support a dissolute life style. In reality, once Dreyfus was introduced to his future wife, Lucie Hadamard, the daughter of a diamond dealer, through the upper middle class Jewish circles in Paris, his life changed radically. He was to become a devoted husband and father, living quietly and contentedly in a family environment.

In fact, what worked against Dreyfus was not simply his lack of comradeship with fellow officers, but his disinterest in social life. For him, the closed circle of his immediate family was all the society he needed. His letters to his wife from Devil's Island reveal a man totally bound up in family concerns and aloof from other relationships. His wife, Lucie, though very young at the time of her marriage, was far from a frivolous young thing who would care to involve her husband in an empty social life. She was serious about music and serious about her religion. The couple had been married by the Grand Rabbi of France, Zadoc Kahn, in a synagogue in Paris. Four years later, held prisoner in the Cherche-Midi prison, after his first court-martial, the stunned Dreyfus would ask to see that same rabbi, a request that was not granted.

Those first weeks of confinement were particularly difficult for Dreyfus. Initially, he had no idea of the nature of the accusation and he was given no chance to defend himself. He had been separated from his family abruptly and had had no opportunity to make provisions for their welfare and safety, nor even to say good-bye to his two little children. Lucie was very strong throughout this ordeal, from the outset working with Dreyfus' brother on organizing his defense and maintaining a calm exterior for the children. During the difficult years of his imprisonment, while Lucie had faith in her religion, Dreyfus placed his faith squarely in the army and justice.

The Dreyfus diaries and comments from those who came in contact with him or his relatives, throughout the many years from his first trial to his return to France for retrial and his subsequent pardon, portray a man who was alternately shy, aloof, cold, or unfeeling—certainly not a person easy to know. His bearing was always military. His allegiance to the army was unwavering and his gift for introspection was minimal. Some people commented his detachment was almost pathological—observing that he appeared to stand outside himself, as though the ordeal he underwent was not truly his own experience.

Those who had worked to free him during his harsh imprisonment on Devil's Island had, with the exception of his lawyer and his family, never met him, yet they were totally caught up in the cause and expended their energies on exonerating and freeing this victim of injustice. When Dreyfus returned to France, his health ruined, looking decades older than his age, his diffidence came as a great shock to them. The Duchesse de Guermantes remarks in Proust's great work, *La Recherche du Temps Perdu*, "What a pity we can't choose someone else for our innocent!" expressing succinctly the dismay of his supporters. Others echoed the sentiment, saying that Dreyfus, except for his religion, could easily fit the mold of an anti-Dreyfusard. Bernard Lazare, the socialist and Jew who had invested much of his time in the cause, was particularly offended when, on Dreyfus' return, he showed no interest in meeting him or other ardent supporters. Many of these supporters were émigré Jews who saw in Dreyfus' plight the reflection of their own treatment in France. They feared for their future, as the establishment media daily ground out stories about Jewish perfidy to inflame the masses. It would have been reassuring to hear in person from the man they were trying to free, but they never received this reassurance. Dreyfus' innate reserve would not permit him to make a connection with these refugees.

Was Dreyfus a self-hating Jew? Was he reluctant to acknowledge his background? His diaries give no indication except by the absence of references to Judaism. He may, however, have deliberately not mentioned religion because of his strong sense of privacy. Many incidents in his life are evidence that he wanted to be judged only on his merits.

Particularly in the army, where Jews were far from welcome, he had kept a low profile, although he had never denied his religion. How could he, when the status system so entrenched in French society was an integral part of the army hierarchy? For other Jews living in France or refugees from the Russian pogroms, Dreyfus was simply not Jewish enough. It was certainly hard to sympathize with a man who refused to see his case in the larger context of religious prejudice and the army's obsessive interest in clearing itself at any cost.

An intensely private man, Dreyfus was truly uncomfortable with the publicity that greeted his return to France, and with the ensuing demands on his time. People remarked that he seemed distant and quite removed from the campaign to restore his reputation; in short, an anti-hero. Yet nearly all the biographical sketches of Dreyfus emphasize the fact that he had never needed people outside his close-knit family. The family was the only setting in which he felt truly at ease. Otherwise, he was uncomfortably shy and could appear cold and indifferent to those who knew him only casually.

Despite his innate shyness and remoteness, he was, nonetheless, extremely grateful to Émile Zola when he returned to France for his second trial and learned of his efforts on his behalf. Years later, Dreyfus insisted upon attending his funeral, although problems of crowd control were expected. Zola had died in a suspicious household accident and rumors that it was no accident sparked public anger. Nonetheless, Dreyfus begged the widow to permit his attendance. She, of course, was worried about possible violence disrupting the funeral cortege and the ceremony, but agreed at the last moment. That day was uneventful, but Madame Zola eventually proved to be right when six years later upon the transfer of Zola's ashes to the Pantheon, a man in the crowd took aim and shot and wounded Dreyfus, who was present at the ceremony.

The contrast between the high fever of the Affair and the detachment of its principal character is quite extraordinary. Yet we can only imagine the psychic damage done to an individual kept in solitary confinement in appalling heat and dirt, often shackled, for nearly five years, without proper nutrition or medical care. Dreyfus needed all the self control he could summon merely to stay alive and lucid. His military training was valuable in maintaining his sanity. He established a plan for study and carried it out methodically.

Had Dreyfus' supporters read his diaries, *Cinq Années de Ma Vie*, they would have understood their unwilling hero better. These diary entries reveal a man far different from the cold and unresponsive individual they saw on his return from years of imprisonment. The diary helps us to visualize the daily effort Dreyfus made to stay alive in his squalid environment:

Vermin swarmed in my hut; mosquitoes, as soon as the rainy season began; ants, all the round, in such large numbers that I had to isolate my table by placing the legs of it in old preserve boxes filled with petroleum.

The horrors of years of solitary confinement in a fetid, tropical climate, where for months he was prevented from even looking at the ocean by a high stockade which surrounded his airless hut, provoked a self-discipline that took every ounce of his energy. He refused to complain to his captors or to beg for their consideration. They in turn were under orders not to speak to him and not to show any sympathy.

Dreyfus writes that he often contemplated suicide at the beginning of his confinement, but the thought of his wife and children always drew him back from the edge. The diary entries reveal a man whose universe was his family—an intensely private man whose affection for his wife was boundless. His letters to her and hers to him would appear mundane to some readers, in their repeated avowals of loyalty, their pleas for courage, and their concern for each other. They were very young and had not been married many years. Their mutual constancy seems scripted, but the years they spent together until Dreyfus' death in 1935, as witnessed and documented by their children and grandchildren, are proof of their sincere devotion.

From the beginning of his captivity on the Île de Ré, he wrote of his innocence and the belief that the truth would be discovered. This is an excerpt from a letter to his wife from La Santé prison on January 11, 1895:

...that even now I sometimes think that I am the victim of a horrible nightmare. I do not complain of my physical sufferings—you know that I treat such things with contempt; but to think that a terrible, infamous accusation is attached to my name, and that I am innocent...Oh, not that! I have endured all these tortures, all these indignities, because I am convinced that soon or late the truth will be discovered and justice will be done me!

For over five years, his wife did not miss a day of writing to him, although months would go by when her mail was held up and censored so there was no certainty that her letters would be received. Madame Dreyfus and other relatives were forbidden from writing any details of their efforts to win a new trial and prove his innocence. Dreyfus' situation was the same in that he could not speak directly of his legal problems.

In the last few years, they were given only copies of each other's letters. Imagine the pain of reading personal messages in someone else's handwriting! There seemed to be no reason for the government jailers to impose this hardship on Dreyfus. Could it have been a concern of the military, who had relied so heavily on handwriting in the case against Dreyfus, that they would be exposed? Both he and Lucie talk of feeling deprived by not seeing the familiar handwriting.

In February 1896, he wrote:

> Nothing new to read. Days, nights, are all alike. I never open my mouth, I no longer ask for anything. My speech was limited to asking if my letters had come or not. But I am now forbidden to ask even that; or (which is the same thing) the warders are forbidden to answer the most common place questions.

The cruelty of his jailers and the French government was remarkable for exceeding the limits of required treatment of an officer. The commandant of the islands told Dreyfus that he was to be put in irons, though there had been no complaint against him. It was "a measure of precaution," Dreyfus wrote, "When I am already guarded like a wild beast, night and day, by a warder armed with rifle and revolver!"

His petitions to governmental authorities, always set out in correct and unemotional language were either ignored or returned without comment. He was kept in ignorance of progress on his case. In late 1896, for no apparent reason, he was locked in and shackled every night, waking each morning with his ankles rubbed raw. Later the army would have to answer for this severe treatment of an officer, a clear violation of standards.

What kept Dreyfus sane was his tremendous effort at self discipline and the maintaining of his dignity. He spoke frequently in his letters of the honor of his family. He focused on routine. He worked hard on improving his English. He asked for books and journals, which sometimes took months to arrive. He talked to himself about what he had studied and what he needed yet to learn.

So, the picture emerges, not of a dispassionate and cold individual, but of a man whose military training saved him from madness, of a man convinced of his innocence, but one who had no interest in politics and never considered his case to be a political one.

Although those who say wryly that Dreyfus himself was not a Dreyfusard speak the truth, they lack an understanding of his upbringing and his mental state. The disappointment for Dreyfusards was that their hero did not wish to be a symbol, but simply longed to resume his military career and his family life. Their hero was a bourgeois with no charisma and few social skills. He was not an ideologue and had difficulty understanding the passion of those who thought they could use his case to transform the old social and economic institutions of France. He saw himself as the victim of a great injustice, but not as a representative of any larger issues. He was uncomfortable with the notion of sympathizers unknown to him, so he resisted becoming a symbol in his own lifetime.

In an age of celebrity, we can't understand reclusiveness. It's hard for the public to accept that a hero might wish to retain his privacy and neither respond to nor encourage the public's interest in him. Dreyfus had no interest in notoriety. The media connection has so much impact today that instant heroes can be made through one photo or television image circulated throughout the nation or the world. This mass journalistic phenomenon may actually have begun with the Affair, although the graphic representations of the time were caricatures rather than photos.

In the past, heroes were heroes simply because of their position in the social hierarchy—monarchs, nobility, generals, and politicians. In ancient times, heroes were celebrated for their great deeds. Heroes were legendary, larger than life. Dreyfus did not fit the mold, although his supporters, so intensely engaged in seeking justice, wanted desperately for him to fill the role.

Had they actually known him, had he not been thousands of miles away in isolation on a fetid island, the battle for justice might well have taken another turn. Perhaps they would have been discouraged by his reserve. In the salons, which Dreyfus sometimes frequented after his release, he was conspicuously silent. The reality was that the man was far less interesting than his cause. As it was, he was a hero *manqué.*

A victim is unlikely to be a hero, because sympathy does not necessarily equal respect. Dreyfus clearly did not seek martyrdom. He wanted only that the army acknowledge its dreadful mistake and permit him to resume his military career with honor. His loyalty to the military never faltered and he never contemplated another career.

Despite the cruelty of his treatment—and it would later be found that most of his guards exceeded their task, as did those in the High Command in Paris—he thought he had nothing to fear from soldiers. He remained convinced, against all his experience, there was no conspiracy against him. The obvious anti-Semitism of the army was, of course, known to him, but he rejected it as an explanation of his ill treatment. He felt somehow his superior officers must have reason to believe he had committed treason. He was the last one to support a conspiracy theory. In his mind, he was convinced there must have been a bureaucratic mistake.

It really took the second court-martial judgment for Dreyfus to begin to doubt the objectivity of his superiors and become desperate to vindicate himself, but by then, he was in such frail condition that his lawyers and family begged him to accept a pardon rather than appeal. This time, however, in the glare of world publicity, everyone could see the system of military justice at its worst. There was not even a vestige of proof against the accused. To put it very simply, there was no explanation of why Dreyfus would have become a traitor. No motive could be established. He was wealthy and had no need of money. He had no political axe to grind. Unlike many officers, he had no debts and had never demonstrated anything other than dedication to his country.

At the outbreak of World War I, after several years of convalescence, Dreyfus requested active duty. Since the authorities didn't know quite how to handle this because of his age and celebrity, they gave him a post as an artillery officer under the military governor of Paris.

Dreyfus' son, Pierre, was assigned to a unit whose mission was to invade Mulhouse, where his father had been born and where the Dreyfus family had deep roots. Twenty years after his father had been mistrusted and reviled as an Alsatian, his son would march proudly into Alsace with French troops. In reality, the liberation was short-lived because the Germans staged a counter-attack, but the point was made. The Dreyfus family had proved their honor and their loyalty as defenders of France.

Other members of the extended Dreyfus family eagerly served in the French army, apparently feeling no bitterness toward the institution that had orchestrated the vendetta against their relative. Looking at the genealogical chart in Michael Burns' book on the Dreyfus family, World War I appears to have been a slaughterhouse for the Dreyfuses, with four nephews killed. This enormous sacrifice, however, would not count for much later during the Vichy regime, when all Jews were suspect. But at the end of World War I, there was no mention of resentment against France by the Dreyfus survivors, only patriotic statements about love of country. If anything, Alfred Dreyfus, serving as an artillery officer, was energized by the war and wrote to Lucie that his health was good and he had no problem in serving because he was used to deprivations, due to his years on Devil's Island.

Toward the end of the war, Dreyfus was promoted to Lieutenant Colonel and reveled in the fact that Germany "had collapsed more completely than I had ever dared hope." His satisfaction should have been tempered, because the Germans had wrecked the textile factory in Mulhouse that Mathieu had tried to keep going, in the family interest.

This was not the only disappointment the Dreyfus family experienced, for they were appalled by the new era of workers' trade unions seeking rights and benefits, so different from the paternalistic relationship they had cultivated with their employees pre-war. The rising tide of workers' organizations and protests was foreign to their thinking, as members of the middle class. They were not attuned to the new industrializing society; they were frankly repelled by it. Nevertheless, it is interesting to note that Dreyfus was so moved by the Sacco-Vanzetti case in the United States in 1921 that, in a rare public statement, he expressed his view that the two Italian anarchists deserved a new trial.

The Dreyfuses grew increasingly conservative, frightened by the threat of Bolshevik influence on workers. They had no sympathy for communism, which was making inroads in France. Ironically, there was a strong Jewish contingent in the ranks of communists, but they were Eastern European and/or working class Jews, with whom the Dreyfus family had never identified.

The Dreyfuses considered themselves French and this foreign element, Jewish or Christian, was completely alien to them. They had never denied their Jewishness, but the Dreyfuses were capitalists and Frenchmen first. Religion remained a private family matter. The unlikely hero of those who hoped for a France that would return to the revolutionary values of *Liberté, Égalité, Fraternité*, was himself a conservative at heart. Dreyfus was no Dreyfusard.

Dreyfus lived out his life, after the initial phase of his recovery, in the south of France and Switzerland, later in an elegant apartment in Paris, taking daily strolls and quietly enjoying the company of his grandchildren. He was a creature of habit, structuring his life around small tasks, writing every day at his desk.

The grandchildren remember him as quiet and kindly, but suffering from nightmares that disturbed his sleep. They recall hearing him cry out during the night. His health was ruined; he suffered from fevers. He spent long hours alone with his stamp collection. He refused to become a martyr or a public figure. He was as contented as he could be with this slow-paced life. His son, Pierre, who died in a plane crash in 1946 characterized him as one of the "purest heroes of our beloved France." Dreyfus' daughter lived until 1981 and reminded people of her father in her manner and physical appearance.

Between the wars, both France and Germany underwent major economic and demographic changes. Both countries had lost a considerable proportion of their populations to the war. Both their industrial bases had been exhausted by World War I and needed rebuilding. Germany, of course, had suffered even more as a result of the tough reparations agreement at Versailles. Both nations were paranoid about the border between them. National self-esteem was at a low ebb in this post-war period of economic and political instability.

Neither the Weimar Republic nor the French Fourth Republic seemed capable of dealing with the problems before them. Looking back, we can see how the roots of fascism took hold in both countries and soon combined with anti-Semitism to create a threatening environment for believers in democratic government, and especially for Jews.

Four

The Historical Context

It is a crime to exploit patriotism for works of hatred.
—Émile Zola

TO UNDERSTAND THE DREYFUS AFFAIR, one must understand the history of the time period, since the complexity of the circumstances, the roles of the principal actors, and the reaction of the public all can be best explained in the context of history. And these explanations are not of the moment, but must extend backward and forward in time, in order to make sense of the multidimensional variables involved. They mirror the swirling, dramatic forces of nationalism, anti-republicanism, anti-clericalism, anti-Semitism, anti-intellectualism, and the insecurities of a society making a painful transition into the industrial age.

Effects of the Franco-Prussian War

The Franco-Prussian War was brief, technically lasting only from July

1870 to May 10, 1871, but its effects persisted and marked France for decades to come. The impact of the war resonated in the Dreyfus Affair and in French society for years after the final humiliation of the defeat at Sedan. It left two countries, France and Germany, in a serious reversal of power and the reputation of the French army in shreds. Although this was to be expected as inherent to the nature of war, even today there is disagreement as to why France was traumatized for so long and so deeply by its military defeat.

The ensuing German attitude toward France is easier to comprehend. Germany emerged from the war energized and unified. What had been a collection of independent republics and confederations was now one nation dominated by a strong military component, Prussia. It was on its way to being a world power, lagging behind in colonial possessions, but out in front in military might and statecraft, with Bismarck at its head. While France struggled to find a suitable form of government and stable leadership, Germany was solidifying its domestic and foreign policies. In contrast to France, it was becoming strikingly modern in its developing industry.

France turned to Russia for support, but Germany had the ear of the great naval power of Great Britain (partly assured by the blood ties linking the two thrones) and the luck to profit from the historic enmity between France and Great Britain. Rather than rising to the challenge with an all-out drive for modernization of its military and its economy, France was held back by the problem of a rapid succession of governments, none of which was strong enough to exercise power consistently. Yet neither were any opposition forces able to unite and offer an alternative. France was *accablée*—a very descriptive French adjective meaning exhausted or overcome. There seemed to be no strength in the political center. This pattern of weakness continued until the outbreak of World

War I. France, as the historian Eric Hobsbawm calls her, "the mother of European democracies," had a record of 52 cabinets in that time period with only 11 lasting more than 12 months.[1] She may have been the mother of democracy, but she was certainly not the model of political stability. With the civil authority of the Third Republic so weak, the military had a perfect opportunity to seize the initiative.

Alliance of Church and Army

In a sense, the Dreyfus Affair was yet another example of the strong French resistance to change. It can be seen as a last-ditch, establishment attempt to keep France as it had been. A reactionary theme dominated the opposition to Dreyfus' retrial. France for the French, no outsiders, a rural way of life, a deep respect for long-outmoded royalist leanings—although France was now a republic—and an attempt to retain power for the Catholic church in an avowed secular republic. The basically conservative, anti-republican elements of French society were still counter-revolutionary a century after the Revolution, at war against the republican form of government, albeit from within. It was fitting that now it should be the military to wage this cultural war to compensate for its mistakes in the actual war that preceded it.

General Mercier, who was to be Dreyfus' leading antagonist to the end, was a general in trouble after the Franco-Prussian War and Dreyfus was the life preserver he grasped to keep him in power. Finding himself in a difficult situation, being blamed for having appointed a Jew to a sensitive position and eager to redeem himself as a tough commander, he proceeded with the court-martial that should never have taken place. Having chosen this route, he needlessly exposed the army to the scrutiny of the press. Since the press was then overwhelmingly anti-Semitic, it did not seem to be much of a risk. *La Libre Parole*, a Catholic newspaper founded by Édouard Drumont, constantly hammered away at the Jewish officers in the French army, depicting them as intriguers and future traitors. This peculiar coupling of the army and the press would characterize the first years of the Dreyfus Affair, as the High Command regularly supplied their favored papers with information. It endured as a symbiotic relationship that benefited both institutions.

Thus, a case that could have been neatly filed away and forgotten became the vehicle for the political redemption of the army. It served as a clarion call for the country to line up and take sides on the question of Dreyfus' guilt. Divisions in France that had been glossed over now assumed great importance, as the Army and the Church made a formidable alliance against those who supported Dreyfus. The army regarded itself—and thanks to favorable media coverage, so did a majority of citizens—as the embodiment of nationalism, which was identical with patriotism for most Frenchmen. Using its contacts in the press, the army was successful in shaping the controversy over Dreyfus as a case that threatened the existence of the regime, much as the Soviet show trials in the 1930s were used to demonstrate the dangers of disloyalty. From the point of view of the army, Jews were incompatible with their mission; their religion did not fit them for obedience and their business interests could lead them into treason. These myths were perpetrated by an acquiescent press at the beginning of the Dreyfus case and continued as the press, responding to the public relations campaign, repeated the military's view of the situation that the survival of the nation was at stake.

Nationalism has become a byword for 19th-century Europe, describing and defining a great deal of its history. Yet the word covers a complexity of beliefs and emotions that makes it far from straightforward. The province of Alsace is an example of this complexity. In the loss of that province to the Germans, there was a surrender of confidence as well as territory. The allegiance of those Frenchmen who now lived under German rule would always be questioned. The readiness to believe in the treasonous behavior of a Jewish officer in the French military is strongly tied to these attitudes. Suspicion of Dreyfus as a German sympathizer had no logical basis, because he had left Alsace as a child and received a completely French education and upbringing, but it underlay his persecution. Dreyfus seemed to symbolize all the tensions and insecurities of the Third Republic. Nationalism and patriotism were one, no matter how badly understood. The Affair was an egregious case of the perversion of nationalism.

Anti-Clericalism

If anything truly defined the Third Republic—that is, in deeds, not words—it was its anti-clericalism. Of course, this ideology was not particular to the Third Republic, but had permeated French history throughout the Reformation period and the religious wars between Catholics and Protestants, finally culminating with the Revolution. The Enlightenment provided the intellectual reinforcement for the anti-clericals, since the power of reason was the god of the Enlightenment. In the early 18th century, Montesquieu, usually regarded as a moderate and sober commentator on government, wrote a humorous and scathing satire of the Roman Catholic church in his *Lettres Persanes*, in which two fictional Eastern travelers have difficulty in understanding the "magic" of the pope and the beliefs he encourages in his followers. This thinly disguised fantasy mocked the fundamental tenets of the Church. Humanism and rationalism had always been the enemies of French Catholicism, as controlled by the Vatican. In the 19th century, the absolutism of ideas and the absolutism of the monarchy were linked and despised by anti-clerical groups.

American liberal nostalgia tends to see the fight against the Church as Jeffersonian—a plea for religious freedom—but in reality it was nothing like the American variety. The Revolution, fairly bloodthirsty from the first, soon turned very violent in its opposition to the old Order. Along with feudalism, it made war against the Church and its officials. The legacy of the Enlightenment was unyielding opposition to all the Church represented. The revolutionary leaders attempted to suppress religion and deny the Church the basic rights of schools and religious orders. Discussing this struggle, Eric Hobsbawm in his book, *The Age of Empire*, argues that one of the by-products of this was the "militant de-christianization" and the official separation of church and state in France in 1905, a bold, extraordinary step.

According to Hobsbawm, the Roman Catholic church took a hard line against science and reason, placing all free thinkers in the enemy camp. Most practicing Catholics had a deadly fear of freemasonry, which was equal to anti-clericalism in their minds. Americans find this difficult to comprehend, because some of their leading presidents, starting with George Washington, were Masons and we regard their organizations as nothing more than social and philanthropic groups. But for many French Catholics, the Masons were part of a conspiracy to destroy the church. The prejudice against them was as strong as that against the Jews.

The feverish writings of Drumont and other anti-Semites often group Jews and Masons together as enemies of French society. What was the basis of this perceived threat? Why had Protestants long been persecuted with such vengeance? Again, history provides one explanation: In the popular mind, there was a clear connection with the excesses of the Revolution that frightened them, and was not entirely irrational. Yet there was a strong irrational component in the fear of masonry. The word "satanic" was often used to describe masonic activity. Since masonic orders held their rites in secret, the imagination of a not-very-literate population was convinced that somehow Masons were practicing a form of satanism.

The Revolution regarded the Church as an institution to serve the state's goals. It was an arm of the state and subject to the civil constitution. This created a paradoxical situation, in that clerics were expected to act as state functionaries. It soon became very hard to recruit priests. Far from a separation of church and state, this regime amounted to an annexation of the church. It was the state that paid the salaries of the people who served the church. The revolutionary leaders saw the need to re-order society through the redistribution of goods, thus the huge numbers of properties controlled by the Church were high on their list for change. Even many loyal Catholics felt the great wealth of Church holdings should belong to the nation.[2] It is estimated the value of church property before the Revolution exceeded the national debt.

Although the Church's official status had been minimized since the Revolution, in reality, it still controlled education as well as vast properties. There was no doubt that the Catholic Church was a primary force in France. During the Napoleonic era, Napoleon continued the centralization of power of the old monarchy in the form of a dictatorship. His Concordat, an agreement regulating relations between the Church and state, set limits to Church authority, but at the same time gave it status as "the religion of the majority." However, Protestantism and Judaism were also acknowledged in this document.[3] A secular regime in a Catholic country was something of an anomaly in Europe, but whether it actually functioned as such is problematic. For example, priests were supposed to take an oath to support the state, although this was counter to the principles of the Vatican. It is unclear how many actually did obey the civil command.

By the time of the Orleanist era (1830–1848), a Catholic revival was in progress. Under the Falloux Law of 1850, described as the greatest clerical victory of the 19th century, the church obtained the right to operate secondary schools. Religious education was also required under the law. As Catholic power increased, so did opposition to it, with the formerly rational freemasons participating in a struggle characterized by violence and bigotry. This polarization of believers and non-believers would poison the atmosphere in French politics for generations. The battle between Dreyfusards and anti-Dreyfusards flourished in the ongoing and bitter controversy.

One of the books of Zola's trilogy, *Vérité*, was published in 1901. Its anti-clerical theme featured a Jewish schoolmaster (a thinly disguised stand-in for Dreyfus) who suffered a terrible injustice at the hands of the stupid clergy. It fit the mood of the political leadership and, as we know, Zola's writings had tremendous incendiary potential. The day after "J'Accuse," was published, riots broke out across France and Algeria; there was serious violence against Jews and Jewish-owned property.[4] It was truly a pitched battle between the right and the left, the religious and the secular. By the turn of the century, anti-clericalism peaked, with the introduction of many laws restraining the church and a secular victory in the elections of 1902.

Since the Dreyfus Affair lasted past the turn of the century, acknowledged or not, it had an impact on these laws restricting religious orders (associations) and the ongoing polarization between clerical and republican voters. The Church became more strongly identified with right-wing politics, while the Third Republic moved more to the left as a response to what their leaders felt was a threat to republican government. By 1904, France had banned all teaching by religious congregations and had broken off relations with the Vatican. An equally divisive issue, though affecting a far smaller number of people, was that of religious identification cards for military officers. Finally, in July of 1905, a separation law was passed in an attempt to end the ambiguity of the church-state relationship.

In his study of the Third Republic, Maurice Agulhon remarks that the status of Catholics in that period is often hard to define because it is so contradictory. Although the Church portrayed itself as "exiled in its own country,"[5] a victim of hostility on the part of the state, Agulhon questions this assessment. The Third Republic repeatedly attacked the Church for its subservience to Rome and for the poor quality of its teaching orders. Yet the Church was undeterred from waging its constant struggle against the government for control of education. This was the major battleground of the Third Republic and its adversaries. In an age of monarchy, the government's stated goal was to indoctrinate children to republicanism in the schools and to fight superstition. The Jesuits were the target of the Third Republic attempt to free education from sectarian influences. The so-called unauthorized teaching orders were to be supplanted by lay teachers, both men and women. However, the Church presented an obstacle to this goal and stood its ground, with the backing of its loyal constituencies. The Jesuits were banned officially, but continued to run their schools. Despite serious and constant clashes over the government's active policy of anti-clericalism, the Church remained a strong influence in the urban and provincial press and in rural French society, proving how deep the roots of Catholicism had been planted in the culture.

There was one Catholic "association," founded by the Augustin Fathers of the Assumption, which was part of a mystical movement that gained mass popularity after the Franco-Prussian defeat. This movement resembled bible-thumping revivals in the United States. They attracted huge audiences, encouraged visits to "shrines," and generally were out to ignite the enthusiasm of the lower classes. One way to do this was to frighten the people into an extreme form of anti-Semitism, although most of their audience had undoubtedly never encountered a Jew. The Augustins published one newspaper exclusively dedicated to pilgrims and another, the famous *La Croix*, which prided itself on being the "most anti-Jewish newspaper in France."

In taking on the Church, the Third Republic made a host of articulate enemies—many of whom were to become leading anti-Dreyfusards. Édouard Drumont, a writer, was the most famous. Well before the Dreyfus case, he had published a scurrilous, two-volume book against the Jews—*La France Juive*. Considering the infinitesimal number of Jews in France (an estimated 40 to 50 thousand in mainland France at the time of the Dreyfus Affair, or .02 percent of the population), it took quite an act of imagination to propound his theory that the Jews were conspiring to take over France.[6] Yet Drumont's conspiracy theory was widely believed and his book was a best seller, prompting him to found a newspaper, *La Libre Parole* in 1892, in which he published lists of "secret" Jews. The paper was dedicated to "the defense of Catholic France against atheists, republicans, Free Masons, and Jews." The virulence of the language of Drumont's articles and the insistence that the economic troubles of those who had lost money when the Union Générale bank failed (supposedly because of Jewish actions), contributed to the passionate anti-Semitism of the readers of *La Libre Parole*. Profiting from the economic uncertainties of a country in transition from a rural to an urban economy, Drumont blamed the Jews for economic distress in the provinces. He was unsparing in his characterization of the Jews as money-grubbing, sinister people, who were out to destroy France for their own ill-defined purposes.

It must be said that the pope himself did not take an active position in support of anti-Semitism, though he did not speak out against it. Leo XIII became pope in 1878 and was more moderate and progressive than his predecessor. He was troubled by the Dreyfus Affair and by the calumnies in Drumont's publication, but was reluctant to take a stand because of the complicated diplomatic game he was playing in Europe.

For the Church, the subtleties of European politics had higher priority than an injustice perpetrated against one man. Leo XIII had no wish to go against the French government publicly.

By 1898, however, the Pope began to worry that his policy of "appeasement" with France might backfire, as the evidence of Dreyfus' innocence mounted. The official Vatican position developed as one of distance, saying that Catholics should not meddle in a judicial matter. The Pope tried, in this instance, to separate religion from politics and remained silent, except for criticism of Drumont's more sensational propaganda against the Jews. Nonetheless, the Italian press did not follow the papal directive and continued to portray Zola as a pornographer, and the whole Affair as a plot by Jews and Masons against the army and the Church.

When Dreyfus was court-martialed the first time, Drumont and his adherents could not overlook a case of suspected treason with a Jew as the chief suspect. It provided an opportunity for them to stir up the public, which Drumont did brilliantly. His scape-goating of the Jews reached a hysterical point during the Affair and continued for years after by sympathizers in print, in caricatures, and in protests. It is difficult for us now to envision the viciousness of this campaign against the Jews, until we look at the graphics of the time. These are frightening visual expressions of pure hatred. It was a no-holds-barred attack.

European Imperialism

Just as their loss in the Franco-Prussian War was a blow to French esteem, so was their distant-second-place position in the race for colonial possessions. In the constant maneuvering for domination in the latter part of the 19th century, Great Britain had an enormous lead. At the Congress of Berlin in 1878, the major countries of Europe met to decide what to do with the Balkan region, then controlled by Turkey. They were worried about Russian expansion into the region and wanted to redraw the boundaries as quickly as possible. France, fresh from its defeat by the Germans, was present but not a major player. Britain got Cyprus and Russia was kept at bay with a strip of Bessarabia.

More important was the famous Berlin Conference of 1884-85, where, once again, the imperial powers gathered to redraw or reconfirm the colonial possessions in Africa that would hugely influence the economic future of the great powers, giving them raw materials and markets for their manufactured goods. Economic domination was the new form of imperialism. In this effort, too, Great Britain remained in the lead, although France managed to acquire a firm base on the African continent that lasted through the Second World War. At Berlin, they were able to establish eight colonies in East Africa and Equatorial Africa.

In *The Age of Empire*, Hobsbawm writes that between 1876 and 1915, about one-quarter of the globe's land surface was distributed or redistributed as colonies among a half-dozen nations. Great Britain increased its territories by some 4 million square miles, while France added 3.5 million. There was a tremendous competition for colonies for reasons that went beyond economics and had to do with status, so important in the psychology of nationalism. Those nations who came late to the game often proved to be the most rapacious; King Leopold of Belgium provided an example of particularly vicious treatment of native populations.

Algeria, of course, was France's prime possession and would remain so until well after the war. The substantial community of French settlers living in Algeria grew steadily over the years and provided a solid base of support for conservative French politicians. These settlers also constituted a hard-core anti-Dreyfusard group. Algeria was a center for anti-Semitism that had been on the rise since the Cremieux decree of October 14, 1871 (after the Franco-Prussian War), which granted citizenship to all the Jews of Algeria (there were 50,000). The announcement of this decree set off a wave of destruction of Jewish property. One of the leaders of the violence took a line from Thomas Jefferson and said he would "water the liberty tree with Jewish blood." This man, Max Regis, was soon to become known as "Jesus Regis" and to found a newspaper called, *L'Anti-Juif*. Algerian anti-Semitism persisted for the following decades; four of the six Algerian deputies in the elections of 1898 joined the "anti-Semitic caucus" in the Chamber.[7] Uprisings against the Jews in Algeria were more violent and more prolonged than those in France. The colonists were more French than the French, as they were to prove later in the Algerian revolution of 1954.

Economic Distress: The Collapse of the Union Générale Bank and the Panama Canal Scandal

An important factor in the rising anger against the Jews was the crash of the Union Générale Bank in 1882. The Bank had been organized by Catholics as a counterweight to the existing banking system, which many believed was controlled by Jews and Protestants, though the Catholic bank director himself had trained under the Rothschilds. The Union Générale was at first a success, but a period of economic downturn and bad investments on the part of the director resulted in serious losses for investors. There was no evidence of any connection between these losses and Protestants or Jews or officials of the Third Republic, but the rumors spread of an anti-Catholic plot. The Rothschilds, too, were always targets of popular hatred when it came to matters of finance. In any event, the crash added to the widespread mistrust of the Third Republic. It reinforced one of the most powerful of the Jewish stereotypes, which was their attitude toward money, manifest in their economic roles as pawnbrokers and bankers.

Ferdinand de Lesseps was a great French hero, having built the Suez Canal in 1871. He had a reputation as a visionary in the French mind, so when his next effort—the construction of a similar canal across the Isthmus of Panama—collapsed financially in 1888, it came as a shock to the public. A massive investigation was called for and followed immediately; the results were an unpleasant surprise. It was revealed that a very large number of important people—members of parliament, leading newspapermen, and cabinet ministers had all been involved in instances of bribery to cover up the financial straits in which the bankrupt company found itself. Since this was a time of economic depression as well, the failure was particularly disastrous.

These widespread instances of corruption were blamed on the Jews, who ran the holding company for the stock issues in which so many small investors, attracted by the romance of the project, had lost their money. These losses were imprinted in the memories of a generation of investors, to the detriment of the Jews in France, because Jewish names were prominent in the financial debacle. One, Jacques de Reinach, in fact, committed suicide, adding to the tragedy (his son was to become a leading advocate and chronicler of the Dreyfus case). This reinforced the myth of Jews out to destroy France long after the event. The indignation of the people who had lost their savings also further sullied the reputation of Third Republic politicians. Many respected republican parliamentary leaders, Georges Clemenceau, for example, were criticized severely and brought down by the Panama scandal.

Socialism

Closely linked to the financial crises of the time was the rise of socialism. The French were no strangers to the socialist philosophy since François Marie Charles Fourier, one of the founders of modern socialism, was a compatriot. His brand of socialism was based on small agricultural communities in which each member would own a share. This movement became the spearhead of Utopianism, which had a strong intellectual appeal. Many small communes committed to Fourier's ideas were founded in the United States in the first part of the 19th century. However, the socialism of an industrial society was something else indeed and was rooted in class conflict, rather than a utopian view of people living in harmony.

Socialism as an economic theory had, of course, been present in history forever, depending on how one defines it, but as a workers' movement tied to an industrial age, it owes its provenance to Karl Marx. As it developed in France, it was a blow against capitalism—an effort to obtain justice for workers exploited in a rapidly industrializing society. The goal was to eradicate the disturbing phenomena linked to capitalism, like unemployment and the gap between rich and poor. Matters like wages, hours, and working conditions were the basis of protests and demands for a more equitable distribution of wealth.

Initially there was little sympathy for Dreyfus among socialists, since he was regarded as a member of the wealthy employer class and not worthy of workers' efforts expended to free him. In fact, there was considerable anti-Semitism among the working class, who viewed all Jews as capitalists and, therefore, enemies. In an article in *Harper's Weekly,* [8] Felix Aucaigne explores the confusing relationship between socialism and Dreyfusards. He says that France appears (in the drive for revision) as "a branch of Bedlam," with major institutions of France responding to the call for revision in illiberal ways.

> The socialists and the anarchists, those avowed enemies of capital, shout and fight in favor of Dreyfus and the Jews, who are in a large part, the owners and representatives of said capital. But, in fact, they give satisfaction to one of their doctrines—hatred of the army.

Dreyfus, on his return from exile, had trouble reconciling himself to acceptance of support from Jean Jaurès, with whose ideas he strongly disagreed. The socialist position evolved during the Affair to a semblance of unity, but later the inevitable split between intellectuals and workers occurred. Finally, the differences between Marxist socialism and the republican socialism of Jean Jaurès were too great to be smoothed over. [9]

It was not that long before—in 1871—that the Commune de Paris had been vanquished in a bloody clash with law enforcement, leaving many supporters feeling they would never see social revolution in their lifetime, and anti-republicans feeling that the French system could not continue as it had been with any chance of stability. However, in a generation's time, the context had changed considerably as a result of an influx of immigrants—many Russian, Jewish, and radical—and a growth in the numbers of industrial workers. By the centenary of the 1789 Revolution, socialism had spread beyond northern industrial France to small towns where workers' councils were elected. Despite this progress in the fight for workers' rights, Agulhon points out that the phase of the Republic in which the Affair is situated was essentially conservative in outlook. [10]

Unions had been legal since 1884, and by the 1890s employees began to experience success against resistant employers. [11] There was a series of miners' strikes that raised public awareness of the workers' plight and underlined the class struggle Marx had predicted. For some, the Republic was too bourgeois to help the workers in any significant way. A law of association was passed in 1901 and in November of that year, the Socialist Party of France gained official status, but the ambivalence within the ranks of the Socialist party placed a brake on concerted action. It is interesting to see how nationalism became a rallying point for anti-Dreyfusards and a divisive issue for socialism, which promoted the broader goals of universal justice. These elements were entangled with the anti-Semitic feelings expressed by the anti-Dreyfusards and workers alike. Later expressions of pacifism further complicated group alliances, as it became clear to many that patriotism and nationalism were inseparable and inextricably linked to support of the army. This created a confusing tableau, to say the least.

Socialism as a force was bolstered by the announced secularism of the government. The abuses of the industrial age gave the movement credibility and universality. Economic depression provided fertile ground for the spread of socialism. Yet the concept of class struggle was not widely accepted in the Third Republic. In fact, the anger expressed by small groups of anarchists proved frightening to many citizens. The impassioned speeches of socialist deputies and the hopes for social progress within the context of a republic were credible, but the bomb-throwers on the streets made more of an impression, and terrified the man in the street. There was a truly terrible spate of anarchist violence. Consequently, the anarchists hurt the socialist cause and received brutal punishment—life sentences or death by guillotine.

Fin de Siècle France

How do these currents in history fit with the light-hearted image of *fin de siècle* France? France and the joys of civilized life were synonymous for people who would never see Paris. Today, we read about the stimulating literary ambience of the Parisian salons. We know about the productive artistic lives of the painters and composers of the time, and we flock to exhibitions and concerts of their work more than a century later.

We admire all the colorful paintings *en plein air*, marvel at the reflecting, glittering blue waters of the Seine, and forget about the grim aftermath of the Franco-Prussian war. Nothing about this romanticized view of the period indicates the darker side of French politics and society that profoundly influenced the Affair.

While Paris seemed to be enjoying a perpetual party, one topic dominated its intellectual life and that was the matter of Captain Dreyfus. Proust, both personally and artistically, was obsessed by the case. Keenly aware of his Jewish lineage, he was particularly affected by the crude anti-Semitism of the reactions to the question of Dreyfus' guilt. In his major work, *À la recherche du temps perdu*, the Dreyfus case serves as a persistent motif running through the book, a topic that pervades the conversation of the Parisian salons. It marks a dividing line for so-called polite society—a line which few were able to cross successfully. The Affair created a precarious situation for assimilated Jews and intellectuals, ending many friendships. Beneath the gaiety of the Parisian social world was a strong undercurrent of decadence and decay. Indeed, some influential anti-Dreyfusards had moved beyond a reactionary to a fascist ideology.

The Political Factor

Could a stronger government have contained the forces that brought about the Dreyfus Affair and polarized French society? The Third Republic endured longer than any other French government, although it never had solid leadership. It continued in power from crisis to crisis. In the space of its existence, it had more than thirty different regimes dissolving and reforming with regularity. What support it had was generally based on negative voting, i.e. better this than any other alternative. But a democratic system requires a positive belief in the ability of its government to deal with problems and a broad consensus on the announced rules of the game. The Third Republic, with its innumerable elections and shifting alliances, never achieved this kind of public support. William Shirer, who reported half a century later from Hitler's Berlin, believes the Dreyfus Affair preoccupied the army to such an extent that it was left behind in the military preparedness race with Germany.

From its inception, the Republic had representatives serving in the legislative bodies whose failed aim was to restore the monarchy. History shows that republicanism has not won easy victories in France. It was not as readily accepted as it was in the United States. Gordon Wright refers to the Affair as a bloodless civil war.[12] One might say it was a civil war in which the military was entirely on one side, in effect waging war against a political system. The Republic was initially threatened by Boulangism and next by parliamentary opposition throughout its existence. Constitutions came and went. The rule of law was changeable. Attitudes toward individual rights shifted as governments constantly dissolved and reorganized. Nothing could be depended on and the public picked up on the underlying tensions of the governmental instability. There were repeated failures to compromise and find a middle ground between the forces of conservatism and the *bloc des gauches*, the Left Bloc.

But perhaps the greatest threat to true republicanism was the failure to contain the military. This was a failure both of will and the constitution. The government should have been in control of the army and not the other way around. The weakness of the political regime was evident in the way the generals dictated policy to the politicians and attempted to cover up their mistakes in the Dreyfus case. Despite the number of former generals who ran for presidential office and won elections in the United States, the president was always in control as commander-in-chief because he was president and not because he was a military man. Although the French constitution of 1875 placed the president in charge of the military, every one of his acts still had to be countersigned by a cabinet minister.

In a speech given on the day that Dreyfus was reinstated in the army as an artillery commandant, Clemenceau, then the Interior Minister, spoke to the question of the role of the army in politics: "We insist that the army keep itself away from public affairs, and we will not allow it to place its hands upon the civil power."[13] It was several decades more before his opinion became the accepted one in France.

The legacy of the Dreyfus Affair was foreshadowed in the words of Clemenceau, for much as Zola and others had represented the strong anti-clerical feelings of the Dreyfusards, Clemenceau articulated the anti-militarist position. This insistence on separating church and state, and the military from the civil, is characteristic of a pluralist democracy. Once the military becomes politicized, as it did in the Dreyfus Affair, democracy is sacrificed. There cannot be a military which is inherently opposed to the constitutional regime. As a thoughtful politician, Clemenceau understood this. In our time, Harry Truman, a student of American history, also realized this truth and took the unpopular step of firing MacArthur in order to establish who was in charge.

As the quotation from Zola at the beginning of the chapter informs us, the exploitation of patriotism can do great harm. The army and the Church, by framing the positions taken on the issue of Dreyfus' guilt as measures of loyalty or disloyalty to France, engendered an environment of suspicion and distrust. The facts of the case were lost in the powerful emotional reaction of these two major institutions, which had long felt threatened by republicanism. The problems for any political system when important sectors are opposed to that type of system, cannot be contained indefinitely. No leader had emerged in the years of the Third Republic to bring people to an understanding of what the system actually meant for the future of French politics and society. Once again, the words of Clemenceau provide insight. He said that courageous men defying tyrants were never wanting in history, but true heroism was the courage to defy the tyranny of public opinion.[14]

Five

The Pitched Battle
Dreyfusards versus Anti-Dreyfusards

To free the traitor Dreyfus would not be so important, but if Dreyfus
is more than a traitor, if he is a symbol, that's another matter.
—*Maurice Barrès*

THE FORCE OF PUBLIC OPINION in France is unmistakable in the battle between the Dreyfusards and the anti-Dreyfusards. It gained impact from Émile Zola, who earned a place in history as the most influential Dreyfusard. His was the voice that counted among the dozens of other writers who had much to say on the subject, proving the power of rhetoric at the turn of the century. However, others, though less well known, kept the momentum of the cause alive in the organization and orchestration of the drive for revision.

In the ongoing contest between Dreyfusards and anti-Dreyfusards, which dominated French politics for more than a decade, Catholics tended to form a solid bloc against Dreyfus. This was to be expected, given the fact that France was a Catholic country and most of the anti-Semitic press was strongly Catholic. Important on the front lines were the parish priests, who regularly repeated from the pulpit the often hysterical calumnies of this press. The higher-ranking churchmen never attempted to halt the flow of vitriol. Equally predictable was the angry reaction of lay Catholics to some of the more virulent anti-clerical statements of the republicans. These statements seemed to offer proof of the need for Catholics to unite against their enemies and, as always, the Jews provided a convenient rallying point. The Affair was bound to arouse passions in those who held strong religious beliefs and those who opposed a role for the church in a democratic civil society. This clear division had been present since the Revolution. There seemed to be no strong middle ground.

Yet there was a minority of liberal Catholics who forcefully advocated Dreyfus' freedom as a simple matter of justice. Some of them were famous like Charles Péguy, the poet and publisher, and Paul Viollet, a respected historian. Their voices made a strong impression in certain circles. Whereas opposition to Dreyfus had a definite populist tinge, the support for Dreyfus among Catholics was mainly among intellectuals and those we would call "do-gooders" today. These people would likely have joined a Christian Democratic party, had there been one at that time, because their chief interest was in economic and social reform. They were motivated by their desire to do the work of Christ in the secular world.

Paul Viollet, for example, spearheaded the League for Human Rights —la Ligue des droits de l'Homme—an organization which promoted individual rights and basic freedoms. Péguy wrote to this point in his book, Notre Jeunesse, when he said, in reference to the Affair, that even one crime, one injustice, one illegality, if accepted by the people, could destroy the social contract and result in the dishonor of an entire nation. It was his sincere attempt to reach the consciences of the devout.

Péguy was an unusual combination of republicanism and mysticism. He sought a moral revolution, but thought that religion and republicanism could be compatible only if both evolved in a humanistic way. As an exponent of both individualism and patriotism, a man who provided intellectual content for Catholicism, he at the same time found comfort in the rituals and traditions of the Church. One thing he could never tolerate, however, on either side of the deep chasm between government and religion, was abuse of power. Accordingly, Péguy did not hesitate to challenge the Church's role in the Dreyfus Affair. He argued that Dreyfus' guilt was "cultivated" by the Jesuits, giving religious sanction to an injustice which he said sickened him and all those who cared about fairness and individual rights. He was subject to verbal abuse by anti-Dreyfusards both because of his insistence on Dreyfus' innocence and his personal belief in pacifism. However, when he died on the battlefield early in World War One in the first Battle of the Marne, he finally and tragically proved his patriotism.

Catholics like Péguy were naturally drawn to socialism as a means of eradicating economic injustice. Indeed Péguy was the publisher of Jean Jaurès' *Études socialistes*. Because of their literary and intellectual interests, Péguy and Jaurès found considerable common ground. Péguy had initially hero-worshipped Jaurès, but Jaurès' forays into politics ran counter to Péguy's natural tendencies to prefer ideological causes to the rough and tumble of party politics. In the end, the two men split over this fundamental difference, but in the earlier years, they were united in their devotion to the campaign to win a new trial for Dreyfus.

The support of Jaurès was very important in defusing some of the socialist sentiment of workers against Captain Dreyfus, whom they saw as a capitalist and exploiter of the working man. Jaurès was able to demonstrate that Dreyfus was a victim of an injustice, who deserved the sympathy of those who themselves were underdogs. The Socialist party itself did not take an official position on the case, but Jaurès persisted in his support, emphasizing the fact that Dreyfus had been unfairly subject to arbitrary action and degradation by the military.

Jaurès was willing to sacrifice ideological purity for the freedom of one man, but he had a hard time winning over less tolerant party members. In fact, he lost his parliamentary seat in the May elections of 1898. With compelling eloquence, he tried to touch the hearts of the "proletariat" by saying:

> We are not bound to put ourselves outside humanity for the sake of remaining inside Socialism....It is the first interest of the working class to hasten the discredit and the fall of those high reactionary officers who are ready to turn their guns on the proletariat tomorrow. [1]

Despite the loss of his seat, Jaurès enjoyed seeing the Dreyfusards triumph in the general elections and was pleased to witness the growth of the Socialist party, with an influx of bright, young intellectuals—among them Leon Blum. That the Dreyfus Affair coincided with the growing appeal of socialism was ultimately a stroke of good fortune for Jaurès' socialist colleagues. Once the case was framed in terms of abuse of power by the military, the movement for revision attracted the support of pacifist groups, who regarded the army as an "instrument of imbecility and continual destruction." [2] The anarchists also joined the struggle for Dreyfus' retrial. It looked as though the Affair had succeeded in inspiring and mobilizing the next political generation, who would leave a strong ideological mark on 20th-century French politics.

Another Dreyfus ally of immense reputation, was Georges Clemenceau, a man whose name remains a synonym with republicanism. He had experienced significant damage to his political career in the Panama Canal scandal, because of his relationship with the financial backers of the disastrous Canal project. Clemenceau was accused of using his influence in parliament to get members to vote for the company to issue more bonds for the construction of the canal. Charges of fraud and corruption were difficult to prove, but Clemenceau's reputation was besmirched and he lost the next election. One of the principals, both of whom were Jewish, was Jacques Reinach—uncle of Joseph Reinach who became the first chronicler of the Dreyfus Affair. He committed suicide and an associate, Cornelius Herz, fled to Germany. This, of course, was sensational news and intensified the suspicion of a plot. Forced out of politics, Clemenceau began a career in publishing.

Even had he not been implicated in the Panama scandal, Clemenceau's own intransigence on the question of reform and maintaining the principles of the Revolution might have ended his political career. He simply could not find the support for abolishing the status quo and transforming France into a progressive industrial democracy. He did not seem to understand the word "compromise," and had unwisely attacked Jules Ferry, a leading republican and then foreign minister, for his policy in North Africa. Ferry, best known for working out a school reform arrangement with the clergy, represented a middle ground which Clemenceau could not accept.

The battle for "revision" was the opportunity for Clemenceau to get back into the political action. Although he was the target of criticism from those who saw him as entirely motivated by self-interest with very little concern for Dreyfus personally, in the small world of French politics the fact that Péguy venerated him as an exceptional politician effectively countered this perception. David Robin Watson, one of Clemenceau's biographers, cites an article written by Péguy in his *Cahiers de la Quinzaine,* in which Péguy states that, unlike Jaurès, Clemenceau did not neglect *la mystique pour la politique*. For this reason, Clemenceau earned the enduring admiration of Péguy.

Auguste Scheurer-Kestner, vice-president of the Senate, was an Alsatian who became a firm ally of the Dreyfusard camp. He was highly respected and influential. Ironically, he died on the day Dreyfus was pardoned—before he heard the news. The fact that he was from Alsace cut both ways; his patriotism could not be questioned, since he had fought to preserve Alsace as part of France, while his Protestantism and support of Dreyfus made him suspect. As vice-president of the Senate, his role in obtaining revision was significant and he was personally convinced not only that the process of justice had been corrupted, but that Dreyfus was innocent.

The man who was the keenest intellect of those who worked for Dreyfus' freedom was Bernard Lazare, mentioned before as an early supporter. As a Jew, he had the least credibility of the Dreyfusards, although he expended his unremitting efforts to the cause. Perhaps because he died young, at the age of thirty-eight from cancer, he is the least remembered of the group. He was recruited early on by Mathieu Dreyfus because he had published a major essay in 1894 on anti-Semitism, which gained recognition from the academic community—*L'antisemitisme, son histoire et ses causes*. It was a historical work, tracing the origins of anti-Semitism and optimistically predicting its end, as Jews became assimilated into the communities where they lived.

It was the ferocious anti-Semitism of the press after the first court-martial that changed Lazare's thinking, much as it had Theodor Herzl's, and convinced him to join the Dreyfus family in their struggle. He threw himself into this effort, ceaselessly writing letters and pamphlets. Like modern Israelis, he was anxious to prove that Jews could fight and would no longer submit passively to attacks. His outspokenness frightened the majority of Jews, who had hoped to ride out the storm of the Affair without attracting attention. But Lazare persisted in his polemics. The writings of Drumont in particular provoked him into equally angry responses. The outcome of the war of words between the two was a real duel, in which no blood was spilled. Duels between army officers were not unusual, but during the course of the Affair, many duels were fought between non-military men—editors, writers, and those who felt they had been libeled in the press.

As time went on, Lazare became more and more ardent in his diatribes against anti-Semitism and against the inaction of his co-religionists. He was truly obsessed by the Affair. He was, aside from Mathieu Dreyfus and a few family friends, the only Jew to assume a leadership role in the fight for revision.

It is revealing of the historic context to think that those who might have rallied around a fellow Jew were afraid to do so, whereas today identifying with a group is rightly perceived as a means to power and influence. Consider the 1985–86 espionage case of Jonathan Pollard, which divided the American Jewish community, but which at the same time illustrates the political power of groups. Péguy, who admired Lazare's courage, referred to him as a saint—although it is more likely Péguy who was the true saint, to see beyond the brashness and abrasiveness of his friend, Lazare. In the closed circle of Paris intellectual life, these were the most prominent Dreyfusards.

On the other side of the intellectual divide were Charles Maurras and Maurice Barrès, both fervent nationalists. This strong patriotism led them to a violent hatred of Jews, whom they regarded as interlopers in French society and politics. They valued monarchy, hierarchy, the military, and the Church as the best means of attaining their goal of an orderly society. The revolutionary spirit of individual rights was anathema to them and their view of the state as organic and therefore superior to the needs of individuals. Barrès had a theory of the "group self," by which he meant that all truly French people implicitly shared the same view of their country. His logic led him to the conclusion that anyone who was a nationalist was consequently by definition an anti-Semite. This reasoning excluded Jews from being part of the French nation. His statements carried weight in the academic community, as he provided a philosophical basis of sorts to the anti-Dreyfus crusade. In his campaign to purify French society, Barrès frequently used the word "fatherland" to describe the French nation, a macabre precursor to the later rhetoric of the Nazis.

Another was a well-known woman writer of the time, a member of the nobility, the comtesse de Mirabeau, who wrote under the pen name, "Gyp." Her activities in politics went back to the Boulangistes, but it was as hostess to Barrès and Drumont that she gained special notoriety. She saw the world in terms of good people and Dreyfusards, practicing Christians and Dreyfusards. The story is told that in the course of a libel suit, she once gave her profession in court as "anti-Semite."

She actively supported the League of Patriots, led by Paul Déroulède, a strong nationalist violently opposed to parliamentary government, who threatened to take over the seat of government after the death of Félix Faure and the election of Émile Loubet, a republican who vowed to press for revision. Déroulède had thousands of "troops" he could mobilize, but when a commander failed him at the last moment, he was left waiting at the agreed upon location, La Place de la Nation, with Barrès at his side, to witness a paltry few hundred men march forward with a substitute general at their head. Déroulède was then arrested and tried for organizing a coup d'état. The event was an embarrassment to the nationalists, because it confirmed that no matter how much agitation there was by those opposing Dreyfus, the constitution remained intact.

Charles Maurras had founded the Action Française to disseminate anti-republican ideas. Ironically, he was not particularly religious, but valued the Church as an institution of traditional France. He was a dramatic writer who regarded Lieutenant Colonel Henry as a martyr who had spilled his blood for the honor of the nation. The suicide of Henry was energizing to the anti-Dreyfusards, despite the mystery surrounding it. His death suited their purposes and they capitalized on it, to the point of creating a cult following in a very short time. Henry became their hero posthumously and they organized a fund for his widow, which soon attracted thousands of small contributors. Reporting of the time emphasizes how the sympathy for Henry among ordinary people swept France. The mystique of the bravery of Lieutenant Colonel Henry endured for many years in the minds of those who felt he was the embodiment of the soldierly qualities they venerated.

The opinions of the anti-Dreyfusards were the popular opinions, reflecting the prejudices and superstitions against Jews long cultivated by the Church hierarchy. Drumont's style in his publication *La Libre Parole* (see Chapter Seven) and the "evidence" he produced were highly credible to the true believers. His charges against Jews were simply a heightened, more colorful version of what they had been exposed to for years.

These nationalist writings gave people an outlet for their need to blame someone for the difficult economic circumstances in which they found themselves, and their concerns over the economic and social upheavals associated with modernization. A return to old ways was a welcome solution for people feeling uneasy in a transitional era.

For those who responded to the anti-Semitic propaganda in the anti-Dreyfusard press, the fact they could express their most vitriolic sentiments unchallenged was exhilarating. They were ready to believe everything they read that supported their prejudices, especially when they had the approval of respectable journalists. After all, many of these men had written learned books on race and religion "proving" that the Jews would ultimately destroy the French nation.

A century later, the chances that mass media can print what is clearly group libel without fear of repercussions are slight. Civil liberties groups would immediately leap to the defense of the injured parties. The free-for-all circus that characterized the French press in the Dreyfus era would be held to account in the courtroom.

Thus, the Dreyfus Affair served as a litmus test for French society; your position on the Affair was key to revealing your background, your place in society, and virtually all your opinions on a range of issues. Without the sophisticated polling techniques we now have available, it is impossible for us to know if there was also a large percentage of undecideds in this polarized situation. All the historical sources would lead us to believe there was not. Nor do we know whether people assumed positions as a result of anti-Semitism or concern about the erosion of the institutions of the Army and/or the Church and the accompanying fear of republicanism.

What we do know is that the Affair was the single issue that mobilized public opinion. It is reflected in the serious literature of the time, most particularly in the writings of Proust. Although Proust had never identified as a Jew nor participated in politics, he reacted to the case uncharacteristically by organizing a petition for Dreyfus' retrial. The first signatory on this petition was the venerated author, Anatole France. Many other writers and artists followed suit, until the number of names reached into the thousands. Even the impressionist artist, Monet, who had no interest in politics signed, along with André Gide. It was a prestigious list.

To casual observers, it seemed a group of intellectuals with international leanings were pitted against the solid citizens of France. It was a perception that benefited the anti-Dreyfusards, who defined it in dramatic terms as a struggle for the soul of France. In their minds, anything they could do to generate class hostility was helpful to their cause. Therefore, the elitist nature of the small group who spearheaded the Dreyfusards aided them in framing the question for the majority. The view, which they successfully advanced, was that those who would weaken the military could not possibly have the best interests of their country at heart.

In whichever direction one looked, the country was split: rural versus urban, royalist versus republican, clerical versus anti-clerical, socialist versus capitalist, nationalist versus internationalist. There seemed to be no possibility for compromise. If we take the example of the United States in the 150 years since the Civil War, we can see that similar distinct divisions, though long-lasting, are bound to lose intensity along with changing demographics and the passage of time. Has this been true in France as well?

The imbalance in numbers between the supporters and opponents in the Affair was extraordinary. Yet with the advantage of hindsight, we know that numbers were not the deciding factor in the shift in government policy during the extended and bitter campaign for revision. Rather we observe there was a significant response to elitist pressure, intensified by the element of foreign press coverage. The writings of the philosophers, writers, and historians who comprised this elite eventually outweighed the opinions of the common people. Moreover, we have seen that—although the preponderance of the media was initially against Dreyfus—after the first court-martial, a relatively small group of people succeeded in making their case through the media inside and outside France. As a result, Dreyfus was effectively on trial before a wider world audience and this ultimately worked in his favor.

On another level, what was being fought over was something more

universal in nature than the injustice of Dreyfus' treatment—the resistance
of those who were comfortable in the past to entering an uncertain future. This desire to block modernism was not particular to France, but it
had more intensity there than in other countries. The shock of modernism in its international expression was repugnant to a chauvinist nation,
which had always considered itself superior to its neighbors, according
to all the indicators of a civilized nation. The battle lines remained fixed
and seemingly immutable.

In an article in *French Politics and Society*,[3] Éric Fassin, a French academic, discusses the role of intellectuals in the Dreyfus Affair with some
skepticism. He talks about the prominence of intellectuals in the Affair,
but is reluctant to accept what he calls the myth that the Affair marked
the beginning of political involvement by intellectuals. Yet he does concede that Clemenceau defined the word in its "modern currency," and
that the "public intellectual" had become a political figure, signing petitions and assuming a visible role. We have noted the most startling
example of this in the emergence of Marcel Proust as a Dreyfusard, lobbying his literary friends to sign on to the cause.

Whether or not one agrees that the origins of this sort of public role
for artists lie in the Dreyfus Affair, there was a high degree of involvement on both sides of the argument by serious thinkers over a long period of time. Fassin says that this politicization of the intellectual continues to inform French intellectual life. Other questions interest him more,
however, such as the study of intellectual activity from a comparative
perspective, by looking at how it occurs in other cultural settings.

No one studying the Affair would say that the intellectuals, with the
exception of Zola, were the principal reason Dreyfus' cause became a
universal one. When we look for today's "Dreyfusards," we can find them
actively pursuing different causes that engage them corresponding to

the changes in the political environment. Fassin's thesis is that today's intellectuals have far less sweeping interests and are more likely to be authorities (experts) in specialized policy areas. That is unsurprising, as social and economic issues become more complicated, but there are still those like Zola, who are sensitive to larger questions concerning the nature of government and its response to injustice and poverty. It is simply that their voices are not often heard in academe.

In the end, the Affair did not mark a true victory for the forces of republicanism, for the Dreyfusards had succeeded in silencing their enemies only temporarily. By 1940, history would repeat itself and the battle would be resumed, in more brutal fashion, throughout the German occupation. As we shall see, Vichy was in many aspects a replay of the Affair in its assault on reason and humanism (discussed in Chapter Eight). There was no eradicating the powerful social forces that continued to characterize French society—some unifying, some divisive. Now, at the beginning of the 21st century, the legacy of the Affair still resonates in modern France.

Although the battle between Dreyfusards and their opponents was lengthy and well publicized, it remained a battle between notable individuals. Dreyfus' path to freedom and vindication would certainly have been far quicker in a more organized setting. Missing from the political culture was the organizational structure that characterizes a modern pluralistic society. Group politics had not developed as the important force it now represents. The governments in power were not compelled to respond to this sort of pressure. In a open, democratic system, the Affair would have evolved differently.

Imagine this same case one hundred years later. Think about the groups that would have come out in support of Dreyfus: civil liberties groups, lawyers' associations, Jewish organizations. Then consider the groups arrayed on the opposite side: veterans' groups, super-patriotic groups, anti-Semitic, and other far-right groups. The pressure they would have exerted on the media from the very beginning would have speeded up the process, forcing the military to respond to their demands, as reported in the media.

The use of media by groups in a democratic system is crucial to achieving their goals. The combination of public relations techniques and new technology, e.g. the Internet, can create the desired effects with great rapidity. Although Dreyfus was not a man to capitalize on his celebrity, many of his advocates would have been more than willing to face the camera and appeal directly to the public.

Furthermore, they would have mobilized their supporters via letter-writing campaigns to the media and to elected officials. They would have organized protest marches and other public demonstrations. Jewish groups in particular, no longer worried about possible repercussions, would for the most part have been energetic lobbyists for Dreyfus' freedom. The government would have been subject to pressure far sooner. It would have been difficult to get away with the initial *in camera* proceedings in a more democratic society, in which groups operate as checks on governmental power.

On the other hand, the fact that it took so long to exonerate Dreyfus is undoubtedly a reason his case has left such an indelible mark on France. It was not to be forgotten in the inundation of publicity so common today, such that by the next year nobody would recall his name or what the circumstances had been. The slow pace of the proceedings gave a generation more than enough time to absorb the details. The result was that the ordeal of Dreyfus was assimilated into the experience of millions of Frenchmen. Accordingly, in a nation where social and economic cleavages persisted, the Affair remained a polarizing factor.

Despite the many modern aspects of the Affair, media coverage in particular, it is safe to say that Captain Dreyfus would not have suffered for nearly five years on Devil's Island if he had lived in an age of more rapid and open communication. The Internet would have been the source of millions of dollars and defenders. Television reporting alone would have saved him years of anguish.

Six

Anti-Semitism in Europe in the 19ᵗʰ Century

It is a crime to poison the minds of the little and the humble,
to exasperate the passions of reaction and intolerance,
while seeking shelter behind odious anti-Semitism.
—*Émile Zola*

ANTI-SEMITISM IS OLDER than the death of Christ, for it can be traced without a break in the millennia of history of the Jewish people. In more recent centuries, it has been significant in determining national and theological policy, although it has varied by country and in intensity over time. Europe, the major center for Jewish population in the Diaspora, exemplifies the many forms of anti-Semitism. At its worst, anti-Semitism has a murderous aspect. It is expressed in government policy and in institutionalized persecution or, in extreme cases, outright annihilation of the Jews—what we call genocide today. Sometimes the policy serves as a means of generating fear and, consequently, popular support from those who are not on the death lists. An example of this kind of anti-Semitism in the 19ᵗʰ century would be the infamous Russian pogroms.

There is some academic disagreement about the possibility of drawing a line between racial and religious anti-Semitism. Racial anti-Semitism is the pseudo-scientific belief prominently fostered in the 20th century by Hitler that Jews are not Aryans and, therefore, are unacceptable in European society. Religion is not a factor. The Jews are to be hated because they are believed to be a different racial strain, which would contaminate the purity of those counted as Aryans.

But for some people, Jews are hated and reviled because their religion is not Christian. The "blood libel" taught over many years by the Catholic Church is that the Jews are Christ killers and thus must bear the guilt of his death throughout the centuries. From this teaching arises countless myths centered on blood, one being the Jews' thirst for Christian blood to the degree that they murder Christian children. Sanctioned by the Church over centuries, these stories gained legitimacy and have resulted in periodic waves of violence against Jews.

Other less violent and common forms of anti-Semitism, some legal, others social or economic, are the exclusion of Jews from landowning, particular professions, public office, and citizenship. These laws and customs narrowed the possibilities for Jews to earn their livelihoods and placed many of them in the despised business of money-lending, forbidden to Christians by their interpretation of the Bible.

The impossibility of Jews becoming citizens in many countries also made them outcasts in the countries where they resided. The fact that they could not own land put into question their loyalty to a particular nation, since they supposedly lacked a stake in society. In many countries, Jews were forced into ghettos and made to live apart from Christians. Ghetto life was typically unsanitary, crowded, and circumscribed by laws such as curfews and prohibitions against consorting with non-Jews.

Even in countries where Jews were neither threatened nor isolated physically, they were frequently kept out of the mainstream. In France, perhaps the country with the least institutionalized anti-Semitism in the 19th century, the army was generally out of bounds for Jews. Its leaders pursued a definite anti-Semitic policy by permitting very few Jews to obtain officer training and, accordingly, military careers. Dreyfus was one of a handful of officers in the French army at the end of the 19th century. The environment was not pleasant; there was a fair amount of harrassment among officers, as illustrated by the frequent duels fought between Christians and Jews. The patriotism of Jewish officers was often openly questioned in the media. The army found a useful ally in the Catholic church, which we know was virulently anti-Semitic in its teachings and persisted in stirring up the prejudices of ordinary Catholics against Jews.

Economics also influenced anti-Semitic feelings, because of the image of the Jew as a money-lender and loan shark. Ironically, in contrast to the stereotype of a greedy and avaricious people, by mid-19th century, many Jews had become associated with socialist movements, identifying with workers and encouraging revolution against the established order. Unfortunately, their interest in workers' rights contributed to the perception of them as internationalists who did not place their nation first; bringing the sad paradox full circle, Jews were thus mistrusted as selfish capitalists, who exploited the poor, by many in the working class. Whether perceived as money-hungry capitalists or unpatriotic socialists, they were not welcome in French society.

If ever a case encapsulated the history and social divisions of its time, it was the Dreyfus Affair. Dreyfus, the defendant, had the bad luck to be in the wrong place at the wrong time. He was the perfect fall guy for an embarrassed French military establishment and the target of the right-wing elements of French society, who felt most disgraced by the defeat in the Franco-Prussian War. They would support the army no matter the cost to truth or justice. Dreyfus' particular predicament activated all the fears and resentments of an insecure nation that felt threatened. The Affair showed a great European nation at its worst and, for years after, harmed France's reputation on the international scene.

In the end, no one truly profited from the drawn-out battle to prove a man's innocence. Dreyfus lived out his life, a prematurely old man, broken in health and spirit, taking small consolation from his vindication. The French army never recovered its reputation and the conservative groups in France only hardened their positions as time progressed. When the Germans marched into Paris in 1940 they found a depleted nation, badly split and morally exhausted. The path to Vichy was made easier by the failure of the French to find a national consensus and stand firm against the Germans.

William Shirer, writing about the fall of France in 1940, says the French were ready, even anxious, for fascism.[1] Envision a nation so weary and worn down, it would welcome fascism as a solution to its problems and choose surrender as the way out of its difficulties. There were those who reasoned that resistance was wrong because it would perpetuate a defunct political system, the Third Republic. The Jewish population would suffer horribly from the relative ease with which the French collaborated with their occupier. What can possibly explain this fact? The Affair provides some clues.

France, more than one hundred years after the Affair, still exhibits many of the prejudices of that earlier time: an implicit test of "Frenchness" for its citizens, an adverse reaction to anything different or foreign, finding it threatening, whether it's McDonald's or the "debasement" of the French language by English words, a cumbersome legal system where the burden is on the defendant to prove his innocence, and a need to re-trieve past glory—all these characteristics still weigh heavily in France at the beginning of the 21st century. At the opening of a new exhibit at the Musée d'Art Moderne in Paris featuring foreign artists based in Paris, there was a debate on whether "Jewish" art existed as such. Some crit-ics saw Jewish artists contributing to France's "cultural bastardization."[2] Whether there is sufficient anti-foreign feeling to pose a threat to the social fabric, as it did in the Dreyfus case, is important to consider.

At the beginning of the 19th century, Jews were optimistic about their future in France. The Revolution seemed to offer promise for a peaceful life[3] not possible in other European countries. On August 26, 1789 the government issued the Declaration of the Rights of Man which con-tained this sentence: "Let there be neither Jews nor Christians except at the hour of prayer for those who pray!" This was an exceptionally pro-gressive sounding statement. Emancipation certainly fit the principles of the Revolution and was a clear break with historic tradition, which had not favored the Jews.

In December 1789, a member rose in the National Assembly to say something a bit more complicated and difficult to grasp than the inspi-rational rhetoric of the Declaration: "To the Jews as individuals—every-thing; to the Jews as a group—nothing. They must constitute neither a body politic nor an order; they must be citizens individually." This pro-nouncement was a thinly veiled warning against the pluralism rejected by the French in the coming century. Yet during the Revolution (1791), the Jews of France had become full citizens and thus were able to maintain both their religion and their Frenchness. France was the country which gave Jews a legal status unprecedented in European history. In exchange, the nation received the loyalty of a grateful Jewish community.

This guarantee of rights was a major break with the treatment of Jews in the rest of Europe. Catherine the Great of Russia, for example, had forced Jews to live within the Pale in 1791 (coincidentally the same year French Jews received citizenship). Ghettos were also well established in the provinces that would later make up modern Italy. As late as the 1860s a case of the kidnapping of a Jewish child by the Church in Italy presided over by a so-called liberal pope would make world headlines and result in a bitter political conflict that pitted France and Britain against the Vatican. It was unfortunately not a unique incident, since Christian servants in Jewish households would occasionally baptize their charges in the hope of saving their souls. Yet the details of this story of child snatching read more like a medieval fable than a 19th-century reality. Despite pressure at the highest diplomatic levels from many European countries, including France, the child was never returned to his family. In fact, he became a favorite of the pope and received an education to prepare him for the priesthood, in which he served for the rest of his life; he died in Belgium shortly before World War II.

For Jews, the French Revolution was a truly revolutionary and positive event; they admired its goals of freedom, equality, and brotherhood. According to the Grand Rabbi of France, Zadoc Kahn of Nimes, "[It] is our exodus from Egypt...our modern Passover."[4] This high-flown language seemed removed from the reality of the daily lives of ordinary Jews, although it came from their spiritual leader. What kind of freedom were the Jews to expect, many of whom had been in France since the 15th century? It was unclear. Would they gain and retain the civil rights of full citizens? Or would the ideology of Frenchness, which discouraged ethnic and religious differences, prevail?

From the perspective of the relationship of Jews to the state, the policy of consistories developed at the beginning of the century and strengthened in the Napoleonic era is revealing. Napoleon expected Jews (and Protestants) to use these organizational structures to set limits for their participation in politics. The consistories were self-governing bodies which regulated religious practices within the Jewish community and dealt with internal problems, but required neutrality on political questions (except the Jews were supposed to support national policy, such as recruiting men for the army).

Essentially the consistories resulted in Jews speaking with one voice through their leaders and agreeing to follow French policy, in exchange for the freedom to practice their religion and maintain their customs. It was a means of quieting potential opposition to the regime. This was, of course, in Napoleon's interest. It was not a separation of church and state as a principle of the Enlightenment, but a way of controlling religion by removing it from politics. This low-profile strategy suited most Jews very well, for it permitted them to continue with their businesses and professions without interference. These Jews were mostly of the bourgeoisie and if there were economic difficulties within the community, they felt they could handle them privately.

However, the relatively undisturbed life in a homogeneous community was not to last. Changing demographics help to explain why. Many refugees from the programs in Russia fled to France in the late 19ᵗʰ century, stirring up still more animosity toward foreigners. Czar Alexander I, who governed Russia from 1801 to 1825, had actually liberalized policies for Jews, permitting them entry into jobs and schools they had not had before. However, he backed away from these policies and his successor, Nicolas I, began to drive Jews back into the Pale and conscript young Jewish men into the military—some mere children whose parents desperately attempted to hide them from the Czar's agents. In undemocratic societies like Czarist Russia, people were entirely at the mercy of the sovereigns, for there was no organized opposition to come to their aid. Emigration was the only answer.

By the time of the Dreyfus Affair, anti-Semitism had reached great proportions in Russia and terrorized Jews were fleeing from pogroms in Kiev and Odessa. Laws passed in 1882, called the "May Laws," established a horrendous equation—one third of the Jews would be permitted to emigrate, one third would be converted to Russian Orthodoxy, and one third would be starved. Moreover, the ritual murder myth spread rapidly in Russia, so that the common people were genuinely fearful of Jews. Unsurprisingly, there was a strong correlation between the level of ignorance and the intensity of the fear.

Even though the Catholic Church reviled them as Christ killers, Jews felt a great allegiance toward France. There were periods when they lived relatively undisturbed by their neighbors, but this persistent and irrational accusation, along with others like the "blood libel," hardened into ideology after the Franco-Prussian War. The repercussions created a malaise largely unreported in the writings and stereotypical images of an untroubled *fin de siècle* France. The everyday reality was a far cry from the frivolity of the French theater and music halls.

The French economy was not making a smooth transition to an industrial society and there were severe dislocations, forcing rural people to crowd into the cities looking for work. As Bernard Lazare said in 1894 in his book *Anti-Semitism: Its History and Its Causes*, "The hostility against the Jews which was formerly rooted in sentiment, now became philosophical...Anti-Judaism had become anti-Semitism."[5] It had developed a theoretical basis. It was in this hostile environment that Captain Dreyfus was later tried and convicted.

The time was ripe for an aptly named Anti-Semitic Congress, which convened in Dresden in 1882. Several European nations were represented, although France did not send delegates. There were no more than 80,000 Jews in France (out of 38 million French) at the time of the Dreyfus Affair, plus 45,000 in Algeria, out of a total of nine million Jews in Europe. But immigration after the Franco-Prussian War increased geometrically, mainly from Alsace-Lorraine and Eastern Europe.[6] French Jews were generally not observable as such. Their religious practices or their dress did not make them noticeable. In fact, they much more identified with French culture than Jewish communities in other countries did with the cultures of those nations. It was ironic that this eagerness to assimilate would be of no help to them during the Dreyfus years, or many years later in occupied France during World War II.

Along with the influx of Eastern European Jews came a wave of Alsatian Jews. Of the more than 70 thousand Jews living in France in 1840, two-thirds lived in Alsace-Lorraine. Between 1870 and 1880, 50 thousand Alsatian Jews fled to Paris, while others emigrated to Algeria. An Alsatian Jew was a perfect target for the disgrace the French felt about their defeat by the Germans.

Strong feelings of nationalism would not permit there to be a traitor in the army, the most chauvinist of institutions. No French officer would betray his country; therefore, it had to be someone who was not "really and truly" French. The Army could not afford to be further humiliated. The 19ᵗʰ-century emphasis on nationalism worked against the Jews, whose loyalty to a particular country was readily questioned.

The majority of French Jews, comfortably well-off and reasonably secure socially, had no interest in Zionism. In fact, they found it threatening to their status, because it reinforced the prejudices of those who believed Jews to be less than French and laid them open to criticism as internationalists. For the established Jewish community, it was impossible to be both French and Zionist, because Zionism preached a return to the land of their forefathers and they were perfectly content to stay in France. Zionism was an import of the Eastern European Jews and a disturbing phenomenon foisted upon them, despite their being entirely out of sympathy with its goals. The Russian emigrés were an embarrassment to the Jewish establishment, a group of people they preferred not to acknowledge. The Affair, far from raising consciousness on this touchy issue, was regarded as ended when Dreyfus was "rehabilitated." The Jewish bourgeoisie was glad to close the books on a matter, which seemed to run counter to their interests and their desired image.

The reaction of the "original" French Jewish community of assimilated Jews was comparable to that of the German Jews in the United States when confronted with public matters that were connected to poor Jews, like social services for immigrants. They would have preferred that these matters be taken care of quietly, out of the public view. Similarly, the views of assimilated Jews on Zionism were akin to the Dreyfus Affair reaction—it was safer not to take any public stand on the issue. Supporting a Jewish homeland would make them suspect on the question of nationalism. Yet Lucie Dreyfus sent a message of thanks to the Zionist Congress, which met in New York in 1899 and issued a statement of support of her husband. It took the racial laws of Vichy to convince many middle-class French Jews that for anti-Semites, one Jew was much like another and all would suffer equally—that others defined your Jewishness for you. Theodor Herzl, the founder of the Zionist movement, had learned this lesson at the degradation ceremony of Dreyfus.

In the popular mind, the Jew became the symbol of the intellectual and the internationalist—both suspicious types far removed from the soil and tradition, which were tangible and could be trusted. The land was not the Jew's, no matter where he went. This, of course, was due to the laws prohibiting Jews from owning land for agricultural enterprises beyond feeding their families. What had inspired the young Theodor Herzl, reporting for his newspaper in Vienna on the first stage of the Dreyfus case, became more true as the century entered its last years. That was the need of a scapegoat for those troubled by modernization. Herzl saw the case as "the embodiment of the desire of the vast majority of the French to condemn a Jew, and to condemn all Jews in this one Jew."[7] The rise of anti-Semitism corresponded with the uneasiness of people in a transitional era. It gave them an identifiable enemy and explanation for their economic troubles. The French feared economic changes, which in turn produced social unrest.

Along with demographic shifts, the wrenching transition to an industrial society shook the Catholic establishment and many social classes for different reasons. The aristocrats because they perceived their way of life threatened by socialism; the peasants because of new methods of farming and the growth of manufacturing and cities. The Affair was a perfect vehicle for venting their insecurities and finding a scapegoat. For many in *la France profonde*, there was a general uneasiness created by the challenge of liberal values and secularism to the old traditions. It was a time of moral displacement.

A landmark anti-Semitic work was published in 1886 by Édouard Drumont, entitled *La France Juive*. It was violently anti-Semitic and soon became a bestseller. It was a call to the working classes to blame their economic difficulties on Jewish financiers, as well as on Marxists who sought to stir up class conflict. More than any other person or event, it was Drumont who was responsible for rousing the public to hysteria on the Jewish question. His influence in the Affair cannot be overstated.

According to Robert L. Hoffman's book, *More Than a Trial*, "Public eagerness to consume anti-Semitic claptrap was something new, with nothing before [Drumont's *La France Juive*] attracting comparable attention."[8] Drumont's attacks on Jews and especially Jewish officers were guaranteed triumphs for right-wing politics.

In 1889, Drumont founded La Ligue Nationale Anti-Semite and in 1892, the newspaper, *La Libre Parole*, with the help of the Jesuits. Today we cannot imagine giving an organization as blatantly racist a name as an "Anti-Semitic League," but there were no subtleties or constraints on prejudice in the 19th century. Drumont even spread the story that the Dreyfus family had financed the Commune—the bloody popular uprising against the government in 1871. He was a man consumed by hatred of the Jews, denouncing Jewish officers as traitors in the pages of his paper.

One of the standard objects of his attacks was the Rothschild family, although they had lost their railroads in Alsace-Lorraine during the war. Furthermore, a Rothschild chateau had been taken over by the Prussian High Command. Far from supporting the Germans, the Rothschilds had served as bankers to the French in the war. The notoriety of the Rothschilds as wealthy Jews masked the fact that 40% of the Parisian Jews were poor.

The Panama Canal banking scandal gave Drumont another handy target and he extended his campaign against the Jews when his paper began to denounce Jewish army officers.[9] Thus the late 1880s saw a rise in overt manifestations of anti-Semitism. An election poster for a candidate in the legislative campaign of 1889 was unsparing in its language: "Le Judaïsme voilà l'ennemi! En me présentant je vous donne l'occasion de protester avec moi contre la tyrannie Juive! (Judaism is the enemy. In running for office, I offer you the opportunity to join my protest against Jewish tyranny!)"[10]

In his summary of his father's classic narrative of the Affair,[11] Theodor Reinach emphasizes the situation in the French army after the defeat of 1871. He says that a duel referred to as "L'affaire Crémieu-Foa" was the prelude to l'Affaire Dreyfus. It was not unusual for officers to fight duels, but this one was special because it reflected the pervasive tensions within the French military. It was one of a series of duels in which Jewish officers challenged anti-Semites. In this one, Drumont was forced to defend himself. Both participants were wounded. Coincidentally, one of Cremieu-Foa's seconds was Commandant Walsin-Esterhazy, who would eventually be found to be the man guilty of treason.

The critical duel in 1892 was fought between an anti-Semitic officer and Captain Mayer, an Alsatian Jew. The duel ended in Mayer's death and received an overwhelming amount of publicity because there was a huge crowd at his funeral, since his family was very well known. It served as the culmination of a press campaign orchestrated by Drumont against "Israelite officers"—of whom there were only 300 at the time.

Was Drumont a publicity seeker, a man whose desire to control others outstripped his common sense? It is unclear how much he believed of what he wrote, but he certainly regarded himself as a leader of public opinion, with his heated appeals to the youth of France to avenge themselves for all the iniquities caused by the Jews and to wreak serious punishment on them. He had the backing of many church officials, whose language escalated to the hysterical, suggesting that Jews must live outside normal society and that the gallows would be a good remedy for the harm the Jews had caused the French.[12] Whatever Drumont's motives, he had found a willing constituency for promoting his agenda.

The charges against Jews were wild, even extending to their physical appearance. Horrifying caricatures were printed in newspapers and pamphlets inflaming hatred. The ferocity came close to Hitler's race prejudice. In a perceptive article in *The American Historical Review*,[13] Nancy Fitch argues that the anti-Semitic visual images projected in the press of the time were powerful symbols to most people. These images penetrated rural, as well as urban, areas and became part of the mass culture. According to Fitch, the anti-Semitism of ordinary people in the rural areas was an important bolster to the success of right-wing movements. It was easy to juxtapose the peasants, hardworking and close to the land, against the uprooted, unconnected Jews. Anti-Semitic writings evolved into racial attacks similar to the attacks on blacks in the U.S. before the Civil Rights era, playing to popular fears and ignorance. In a chapter entitled "To Roast the Jews," Bredin speaks of the increasing violence of anti-Semitism.

Some supporters of Dreyfus did not want to see the problem of anti-Semitism buried when he returned from Devil's Island for his second trial. "France seemed to have assimilated the Affair. Had the Jewish community at least retained any memory of its passions?" asked Bernard Lazare.[14] These are comments he made about a dinner held for Picquart when he was released from prison. The author protested against the failure to invite early supporters of the Dreyfus cause. Lazare felt he had been excluded because of his pride in his religion. The issue was apparently one with which Picquart's supporters did not wish to be associated. It was true that Picquart himself was an anti-Semite, whose prejudice had only allowed him to sympathize with Dreyfus because of the injustice factor. For Lazare, who felt strongly about his Jewishness and the role religion played in Dreyfus' plight, this attitude was impossible to understand or to tolerate.

When the battle over revision was raging in France, the premier, Jules Méline, addressed the Chambre des Députés, saying:

The Jews who have foolishly unloosed this prepared campaign of hatred, brought down upon themselves a century of intolerance—the Jews and the intellectual elite which seems to enjoy poisoning the atmosphere and inciting bloody hatred.

The Chambre then passed a law, 428 to 54:

The Chamber invites the government to repress energetically the odious campaign...to rehabilitate the traitor who was unanimously convicted by the testimony of twenty-seven French officers and who has confessed his guilt."[15]

This was the state of official opinion at the time, and the consensus of public opinion as well. Jews were blamed for putting France in an embarrassing situation. It was the classic "blame the victim" reaction.

The problem for many French Jews was their fear of anti-Semitism. They preferred to ignore the subject and go about their lives, especially if they were bourgeois. Silence was to be their response. They did not want to be marked as troublemakers. Initially, most of them believed Dreyfus was guilty and had no wish to pursue the matter.

Mathieu Dreyfus, who organized his brother's defense, had to seek support very quietly, because many of his co-religionists feared any connection with a case of treason. They were used to surviving by keeping their heads down. This timidity made the notion of a Jewish conspiracy laughable. Furthermore, they had never identified with the poor Eastern European émigré Jews or the socialist elements who took up Dreyfus' cause. These Jews did not perceive themselves as outside French culture and were embarrassed by the obviously foreign immigrants. Like so many well-to-do Jews, they were assimilationists—as, of course, was Dreyfus.

As we have remarked, the crash in 1882 of the Union Générale Bank founded and managed by Catholics was blamed on Jews. More than half a century later, one of the Vichy officials on trial explained his hatred of Jews because his family had lost its fortune upon the collapse of the Bank. Conspiracy theories abounded at the time, most particularly directed against the Rothschilds in the Catholic press. Drumont had a ready audience for his screeds. His populist appeal increased hostility toward the Jews.

The failure of the French attempt to build the Panama Canal also inspired anti-Semitism when De Lesseps' company went bankrupt in 1889, for there were Jews in the holding company who were responsible for the losses. The scandal spread as the corruption of members of Parliament and the press came to light; the financial losses of thousands of small investors left them looking for someone to blame. Although there was a lot of enmity (and envy) directed towards Jews as capitalists and financiers along with social contempt, as evidenced in caricatures, paradoxically, there was also considerable intermarriage within the upper reaches of French society and the handful of Jewish officers in the Army at this time.[16] Given a multitude of inconsistencies like these, it becomes very difficult to describe French anti-Semitism precisely.

Whatever the reasons, anti-Semitic emotions ran high in France, and scape-goating and occasional violence against Jews and their businesses were commonplace. In his book, *Explaining Hitler*, Ron Rosenbaum quotes a well-known British literary critic, George Steiner, on the Holocaust:

> It is very odd, given the Dreyfus Affair, that [the Holocaust] didn't happen in France. In some ways, it was ghastly bad luck for Germany that Hitler [was German]—it *could* have happened in France. French anti-Semitism had a kind of systemic power and political profit which it didn't have in Germany. Had it not been for Hitler's quote unquote [sic] peculiar genius, had there been a French Hitler, he might have had an even quicker ascent to power.[17]

However, Robert Hoffman says that anti-Semitism in France was less virulent than in other European countries and grew out of the counter-revolutionary Catholic ideology rather than racism. This group of anti-Semites were usually anti-Masonic and anti-Protestant as well. Mostly, they were united in their fierce opposition to the Third Republic. He concludes there had to be something wrong with a political system that generated so much hatred.[18] It is difficult to understand how a political system consistently and publicly undermined by organized groups could endure. One hundred years after republican government was instituted in France, there were those who still devoted their lives to resisting it. For many observers, the Third Republic remains an enigma, a governmental system that had more staying power than power.

A religious movement led by the Augustin Fathers of the Assumption swept France at the end of the century. Shrines like Lourdes became extremely popular and attracted thousands of pilgrims. The movement (mentioned in Chapter Four) had been in the forefront of the battle against the anti-clericals within the Third Republic who rid the schools of the Assumptionist teachers. This reactionary segment of the Catholic clergy taught that anyone who was not Catholic was not French. As Bredin writes, "The brothers of the Christian schools considered Dreyfus' guilt to be on a par with the infallibility of the Pope."[19] This belief fed attacks on Jews, making the myth of Dreyfus' guilt easy to believe. They popularized anti-Jewish sentiment in songs and verses for school children to sing and recite.

Anti-Semitism was the vehicle for the Radical Right to gain popular support, and a strong Catholic media backed the effort. The Fathers published a daily newspaper, *La Croix*, beginning in 1888 as a means of responding to the anti-clerical measures of the Republic. It was more to the right than the Vatican and became a major source of propaganda for conservative Catholicism. In a scathing article in *The North American Review* of October 1899,[20] the author, H.G. de Blowitz, accuses the Church of acting against the law of charity preached by Jesus by permitting and encouraging priests to poison the minds of French Catholics against the Jews. The pope decided to stay out of the controversy. Without a strong Pope to intervene, the French Catholic Church allied itself solidly against Dreyfus.

An important radical right organization was founded in 1899 specifically in response to the Affair. It was the Action Française, spearheaded by Charles Maurras, a leading royalist and intellectual. The major goal was to bring stability to France by restoring the monarchy. Reactionaries had always opposed representative government and the creation of the Action Française in May 1899 was a catalyst for those anti-republican sentiments. Perhaps because of the high esteem in which its prominent founders were held, when furious outbursts occurred after the Cour de Cassation granted Dreyfus a retrial, the Action was left alone while the heads of other anti-Semitic groups were arrested. Its appeal lasted for decades, during which its members were able to produce huge demonstrations against republicanism by means of a network of local organizations and a daily newspaper, also called *Action Française*. Barrès, another anti-Dreyfusard and contemporary of Maurras, was instrumental in linking nationalism with clericalism. This religious interpretation led to his belief that a true nationalist must be an anti-Semite. Given this sentiment expressed by right-wing intellectuals, it is surprising that Dreyfus won a re-hearing of his case.

Maurras enjoyed a reputation as a sound thinker. His ideas were picked up by others and repeated endlessly in the press. How was Maurras different from Barrès, if he was? Barrès was a strong conservative and a member of the academic establishment in his day. He believed in "the mystical conception of nationality" and a theory of "group self," which resembled Fascist doctrine. Barrès was an unabashed racist. He believed there was a conspiracy of Jews to take over lands that were not their own, that they were the natural enemy of patriots. He said, "That Dreyfus is capable of treason I deduce from his race." [21] Barrès could find race as an explanation for all the evils in France. Anti-Semitism was an obsession for him.

Maurras was a strong nationalist, a royalist, editor of the newspaper, *L'Action Française*, extremely xenophobic, and the leading exponent of conservative thought. There was not much difference between the two and they fit nicely with Drumont's mission; he used them as sources for his pseudo-historical propaganda. It was clear to people like Barrès that Dreyfus had committed treason because he was not and could never be French. Anti-semitism was in the air, natural as breathing. Only when it erupted into violence was there any official concern.

Both men, like so many other reactionaries, were still fighting the battles of the Revolution, hoping that France would reject the revolutionary principles and return to her roots. One of their most popular causes was the defense of Jeanne d'Arc—Joan of Arc—whose mythic reputation had been declining in the French educational system as a result of the influence of anti-clericalism. Reactionaries organized students for the cause of Jeanne d'Arc and benefited from the support of parish priests.

In its enduring opposition to the outcome of the Dreyfus Affair, the Action Française was really trying to turn the clocks back on modernity. Once they began publishing their own newspaper in 1908, they ran news stories unfavorable to the Jews in almost every issue. [22] Anti-Semitism was their journalistic meal ticket.

As time passed, many royalists wanted to disassociate themselves from the Action Française because it had become violently right wing and fanatical. They were uncomfortable with some of their tactics and secondary causes, much as American anti-communists wanted to distance themselves from Senator Joe McCarthy. The average membership of the group, vocal as it was, did not exceed 40,000, about 10% of whom were clergy and 25–30% lower middle class. Socially, the movement appealed to the déclassé nobility—it had no appeal for the bourgeois or the working class. But the concern over the expanding German Empire in the years leading up to World War I made the chauvinism of the Action Française attractive to many people who did not join the group.

Tannenbaum says that "nationalist movements all over Europe were having their heyday during the diplomatic crises leading up to the general conflict."[23] He also writes that the political climate was ripe for a nationalist foreign policy in France. The huge publicity generated by the Dreyfus Affair fit perfectly into this context. How interesting that a patriotic, assimilated Jew who had always kept his religion a private matter should be at the center of the storm of anti-Semitism created by the charges against him.

By 1913, the Action Française was agitating for increased military strength and trying to get the public aroused with anti-German demonstrations. They began to investigate instances of espionage, focusing on "German-Jewish" spies.[24]

As we shall see in a brief summary of the Action Française newspaper in the next chapter, the movement abandoned its anti-Dreyfus theme only once and that was during World War I, in the interests of patriotism and the war effort. However, it resumed its propaganda immediately after the war, with attacks on the Treaty of Versailles and Clemenceau in particular. According to Tannenbaum, there was a belief among some reactionaries that all Jews were related to each other, hence, to Captain Dreyfus. Logically then, all Jews were to blame for Dreyfus' treason.[25]

Well into the 20ᵗʰ century, the Action Française was still unreconciled to the final Dreyfus ruling. It remained an odd throwback to another era, calling for the restoration of the monarchy and trumpeting the glory of the army and of Jeanne d'Arc in the between-the-wars period. Perhaps not coincidentally, fifty years later, Jean-Marie Le Pen would also use Jeanne d'Arc as an icon and a rallying cry.

As late as 1931, Action Française still had enough power to force the closing of a Dreyfusard play in Paris after three performances.[26] The old nationalist ideology seemed to regain strength in the depression years, coinciding with the growing support of fascism. The Dreyfus Affair, says Robert Hoffman, writing about the origins of the reactionary group, lasted until the Nazi era as a viable issue for that organization. The sad reality is that by that time, anti-Semites no longer needed a special group to make their case, since they now had institutional backing for it in fascist regimes. It would take a devastating war and inhuman actions by the Germans to strengthen the old argument for a Jewish state. The birth of Israel has its source in the experience and convictions of Theodor Herzl, which, as we have seen, had originated in the Dreyfus Affair.

Seven

Media in the Dreyfus Affair
The Force of Public Opinion

It is a crime to mislead opinion, to utilize for a task of death
this opinion that they have perverted to the point of delirium.
— *Émile Zola*

ANY STUDENT OF THE AFFAIR will soon reach the conclusion that without the media, the case would not have evolved into one of the most important and enduring controversies in France, bridging the 19th and 20th centuries. In this respect, the Dreyfus Affair proves to be the first trial in which public opinion played a major role, making it a truly modern event. For this reason, sustaining public interest in the case was not a difficult task for the press. Its significant political overtones and the ideological nature of newspapers of the day guaranteed them committed readerships. As Barbara Tuchman has said, the media "fed" on the Dreyfus Affair. Everyone had an opinion and would regularly read the press to validate those opinions. Paradoxically, the case connected many groups, even as it simultaneously polarized society.

From the beginning of the Dreyfus "story," the overseas press showed an interest, extending the boundaries of the case beyond the limits of domestic politics. It was undeniably a good story that no zealous journalist could overlook. The circumstances of Dreyfus' humiliation were dramatic enough to merit the attention of foreign correspondents stationed in Paris and to assure them space in their home newspapers. An officer convicted of treason *in camera* and publicly stripped of his military insignia was worth press attention; discussion of the merits of the case would come later, after the initial drama on that overcast January day in Paris.

Articles about the degradation ceremony appeared in both *The New York Times* and *The New York Herald Tribune* of January 6, 1895. *The Times'* story is more complete, giving a blow-by-blow description of the ceremony, the weather, the crowds, the surprising number of troops present (estimated at 5,000). The ceremony held in the courtyard of the École Militaire in bleak January weather lasted all of four minutes, with Dreyfus shouting out his innocence: "You have degraded an innocent man. I swear that I am innocent," and the crowd shouting *À mort le traître!* and *À mort les Juifs!*[1] The story in the *Tribune* is subjective, conveying the passion of the crowd and asserting there was no doubt of the prisoner's guilt. The reporter writes the secrets betrayed were of great importance, although he provides neither sources nor evidence for this judgment.[2]

After the headlines of the degradation ceremony and Dreyfus' life sentence and exile, the story disappeared for a few years in the overseas press. After all, there was no news to report; Dreyfus was well outside the limited communication network of the time. The official story had concluded with his sentence and there were no reporters assigned to Devil's Island to monitor the life of the prisoner in solitary confinement. The army released no further information and the effort to appeal the verdict was not yet organized or publicized. It was still very much a family matter.

As for the French media, the case had reawakened the anti-Semitism of the Panama Scandal a decade back and a majority of the papers were relentless in waging a campaign against Dreyfus, replete with anti-Semitic innuendos. In the Paris newspapers and in provincial and Catholic publications, this often took the form of a generalized suspicion of Jewish army officers. Many of these newspapers had large circulations even by today's standards—hundreds of thousands of readers. Papers printed the names of Jewish officers for no journalistic reason. They talked about getting rid of the Jewish "cancer," artfully combining their venom against Jews with hatred of the Germans. Most stories about Captain Dreyfus featured the Jewish angle prominently, with frightening caricatures and insinuations about the patriotism of Jews, especially Alsatian Jews.

Although later historians of the Affair tended to de-emphasize its anti-Semitic nature, any reader of the press of the time would have to disagree. Anti-Semitism was not unusual in any European society, but the focus of most media coverage and the language that it employed elevated many of the well-known prejudices to new heights, and to an expanded mass readership. It was the leitmotif of the Dreyfus trial in the French press, and there were dozens of newspapers in Paris alone.

Édouard Drumont had the largest following of any of the journalists of the time and kept the issues of treason and conspiracy alive throughout all the years of the Affair. As editor of *La Libre Parole*, he was well-placed to remain in the forefront of the attack. He was completely consumed by hatred of the Jews and served as a perfect rallying point for Catholic groups that shared his feelings. His newspaper was a publication in which the ideologically inclined French could vent their animosity and suggest drastic solutions to the Jewish problem. These suggestions were far from subtle. Some wanted to confiscate Jewish property; others wanted to expel the Jews from France.

Well before the Dreyfus trial, Drumont had appealed to the youth of France, confiding his hope that they would avenge their elders against the Jews. The language was blatantly racist, playing on popular fears. There was no attempt to moderate the message and certainly no fear of prosecution for libel in that day and age. All these suggestions were presented in the guise of patriotism. By 1898, when Zola gave new life to the case with his dramatic appeal for revision, the ground had been well prepared for a strong emotional response from the public.

The second trial at Rennes was the first covered by a global press corps. The growing use of the telegraph was instrumental in bringing this about. Intensive media coverage in France and Zola's impassioned articles had led to worldwide interest in the case. In the five years since Dreyfus' court-martial, it had become a truly modern media event. Most of the stories received page-one placement. What had created the extraordinary interest in the trial? What had caused newspapers from so many countries to send their reporters to Rennes at great expense?

The answer was remarkably simple. It was the fiery rhetoric of Émile Zola that attracted international attention. In addition to his famous "J'Accuse," laying blame on the establishment in France, he had written a series of similar commentaries railing against the unjust treatment of Dreyfus by the French military and the prejudices of his countrymen. His "Four Letters to France" appeared under the rubric "Truth on the March," a title that soon became the slogan for those working for Dreyfus' freedom.

Émile Zola was a well-known French author when he came to the defense of Alfred Dreyfus in January 1898, three years after Dreyfus had been shamed and convicted in the first court-martial proceeding. A writer with a social conscience, he realized that he was endangering his reputation by going public. He was already considered a "pornographer" by many, who found his realistic descriptions of the lives of the poor in industrial society disturbing. His aim was to mobilize support for the cause of the Dreyfusards and avoid the legalisms that had beset the case. He wanted to reach the hearts and minds of the middle class, who were naturally allied with the conservative forces of traditional France. He felt he could appeal to what was best in his country. As a descendant of the Enlightenment and a believer in the principles of rights, he was certain France could be restored to its leadership in issues of social justice. It was Zola who had the insight that anti-Semitism was corrupting to the nation and that continuing along that negative path would ultimately be destructive to the principles of a modern state. The Second World War would prove Zola was right.

Initially, Zola's thought was to publish his belief in Dreyfus' innocence in pamphlet form, but he decided that it was important to obtain as wide an audience as possible, so he went to a Paris newspaper, *L'Aurore,* for publication. That marked a historic moment. Zola's strong indictment of the French establishment changed the direction of public opinion on the Dreyfus case and polarized the country even further. For Zola had attacked in unequivocal terms the anti-Semitism infused into the traditional institutions of France. He presented his arguments as a battle between good and evil, over what was best and worst in the French people. The divisions that hardened at that time persist to this day, although there are now fewer French at the extremes and more of them clustered in the center of the ideological continuum.

How could a literary document written in haste over two days have such power? Would it be possible in a television age to command public attention with a lengthy letter? It seems unlikely, from our perspective in the context of a rapid and overloaded communications era, but the impact of Zola's polemic extended beyond the borders of France to the rest of Europe and the United States. It had a huge and immediate effect. He asked his countrymen to examine their consciences and to rid the nation of the destructive anti-Semitism that permeated the Affair. He pleaded that prejudice against the Jews could easily turn against Protestants or any other minority group, with frightening results for justice and the lofty ideals of the Revolution and the Enlightenment. The rest of Zola's life and the future of French society would be influenced by the response to his militant and highly emotional language.

In his letter, "J'Accuse," addressed to the president of the Republic, Félix Faure, Zola works up to a powerful crescendo of indignation, paragraph by paragraph, as he accuses by name individuals in the army, the handwriting experts, officials in the war office, and attacks the conduct of the court-martial proceedings. As experts on the case like Jean-Denis Bredin have said, Zola deliberately left himself open to charges of libel in every accusation he made and risked his reputation as a popular author for taking the position he did. He wanted to be prosecuted and he hoped the case would be reopened as a result. In his public search for prosecution, he felt he had drawn a line for those with a conscience.

The letter is forceful and unyielding in its language attacking the military. Some quotes will give the tone of the document and reveal why the reaction was so devastating. Zola says quite bluntly that Colonel du Paty de Clam was the chief conspirator. He tells the story of du Paty's actions dramatically:

> It is he whom Major Forzinetti [the director of the prison] represents to us armed with a dark lantern, trying to gain access to the accused when asleep, in order to throw upon his face a sudden flood of light, and thus surprise a confession of his crime in the confusion of his awakening. I declare simply that Major du Paty de Clam, entrusted as a judicial officer with the duty of preparing the Dreyfus case is, in the order of dates and responsibilities, the first person guilty of the fearful judicial error that has been committed…it is he who invented Dreyfus.

He runs to Mme. Dreyfus, terrorizes her, tells her that, if she speaks, her husband is lost....And thus the examination went on, as in a fifteenth-century chronicle, amid mystery, with a complication of savage expedients, all based on a single charge, this imbecile *bordereau*, which was not simply a vulgar treason, but also the most shameless of swindles, for the famous secrets delivered proved, almost all of them to be valueless.

Ah, the emptiness of this indictment! That a man could have been condemned on this document is a prodigy of iniquity....But a document of interest to the national defense the production of which would lead to a declaration of war tomorrow! No, no. It is a lie the more odious and cynical because they lie with impunity in such a way that no one can convict them of it.

...These, then, Monsieur le President, are the facts which explain how it was possible to commit a judicial error; and the moral proofs, the position of Dreyfus as a man of wealth, the absence of motive, this continual cry of innocence, complete the demonstration that he is a victim of the extraordinary fancies of Major du Paty de Clam, of his clerical surroundings, of the hunting down of the 'dirty Jews' which disgraces our epoch.[3]

Next, Zola addresses the iniquity of the army, which rendered a verdict without merit and then asked the nation to honor and respect them. He says they made a "human sacrifice" of Dreyfus. As for the clergy, he says that the government should "clear away this band of Jesuits."

Finally, Zola concludes with a string of accusations, starting with Colonel du Paty de Clam, then moving on to General Mercier—whom he says was an accomplice, at least through weakness of mind, in one of the greatest iniquities of the century—then the generals involved in the preparation of materials for the trial: Billot, de Boisdeffre, Gonse, de Pellieux, and Commandant Ravary. Next, he accuses the so-called handwriting experts, the war offices, and the first council of war. He dares them all to take him to court, which they did within five days of publication.

The day after the publication of "J'Accuse," riots broke out in France and Algeria. Those in Algeria were particularly violent, with extensive damage to Jewish-owned businesses and synagogues. In the elections of

1898, there was a major turnover in the Chamber of Deputies (196 of the 581 members were newly elected,) forcing the resignation of the prime minister and resulting in an expanded cohort of anti-Semitic legislators. This was the Chamber which cheered Cavaignac, the new War Minister, when he presented them with Lieutenant Colonel Henry's forged evidence and asked for the arrest of all Dreyfusards on grounds of sedition. He was embarrassed a few days later when "le faux Henry," the two documents he had so boldly presented in the Chamber, were revealed to be forgeries. At that point, unlike the unbending generals who perjured themselves with their testimony at Rennes, Cavaignac admitted error and forced Henry to confront his forgery. This marked yet another turning point for the Affair and the Cabinet voted to send the case to the highest court in France, la Cour de Cassation, for a decision on appeal.

After the publication of "J'Accuse," Zola became the focus of widespread public attention, coming under the hostile scrutiny of much of the domestic press while gaining a reputation for courage overseas. Years after the trial at Rennes, he was criticized as "not French" by the conservative Maurice Barrès. "Who exactly is this Monsieur Zola?" he asked "The man is not French"—a reference to the Italian origins of Zola's family and a standard nationalist response to "outsiders."[4]

Others like Leon Blum, the socialist leader, thought Zola the bravest man in the world and the letter a masterpiece, undoubtedly because it attacked injustice on such a grand scale. Journalism held center stage.

The articles by Zola and other respected French writers illustrate the importance of rhetoric in the press of the time, which was far more oriented towards ideas and commentary than reporting the news. Journalism then came closer to literature than journalism today.

"J'Accuse" occupies a special place in political journalism. For Anatole France, it was "a moment in the conscience of mankind."[5] Its impact on public opinion was so great that, for the 1994 centenary of the first Dreyfus trial, scholars from Western and Eastern Europe, the United States, and Latin America gathered at Rennes, France, the site of the second trial, to explore the impact. This colloquium, prompted by a gift of 5,000 documents to the Musée de Bretagne by Jeanne Pierre-Paul Lévy, the daughter of Alfred and Lucie Dreyfus, dealt with matters as diverse as Catholicism, anti-Semitism, human rights, anti-clericalism, and the 1900 Paris World's Fair. All the research was linked by the context of public opinion across a broad spectrum of countries. Never had a judicial matter captured the collective imagination of so many countries and become the subject of so much reportage.

In truth, by the time of the trial at Rennes, the world was watching closely and heads of state—from Queen Victoria to the Kaiser, her grandson—were applying great pressure to the French to arrive at a politically acceptable conclusion to what so many regarded as an unacceptable violation of individual rights. After all, France, for many Europeans was the cradle of republicanism and the shining example of the "rights of man," which had inspired so many other revolutionary movements in the 19th century. Reaction to the Dreyfus case as a result of all the media attention was unprecedented, and was strikingly modern in its emphasis on individual rights.

The sense of outrage was particularly evident in England. Even before the case was remanded for retrial, *The Times* of London had broken tradition and published the longest letter ever written to the editor, on October 13, 1898. Of course, *The Times* had received hundreds of letters on the Dreyfus case, but this one bore the signature of the Permanent Undersecretary of State for Home Affairs, Sir Godfrey Lushington, and, as such, carried great weight. Unlike Zola's impassioned plea, this sober letter set out to show, in a ponderous and matter-of-fact manner, how Dreyfus had been unfairly condemned and how justice had been deliberately subverted.

The letter reviewed in great detail the facts of the case. It took more than a page of space in the newspaper, exposing the forgeries and machinations of the army in its desperate efforts to convict Dreyfus. Document by document, person by person, year by year, Sir Godfrey outlined the perfidious behavior of the military and the conspiracy to cover up the truth. The Queen herself believed that a great injustice had been done and it is probable that she acquiesced to the publication of this letter by a Cabinet member. She told her prime minister that she "was too horrified for words at this monstrous, horrible sentence.... If only all Europe would express its horror and indignation! I trust there will be a severe retribution."[6] Many cynics have remarked that the Dreyfus Affair gave Britain a chance to vent its dislike for France in a principled and sanctimonious way.

According to Bredin:

> By the end of the year 1898, the boundaries separating the Dreyfusards and the anti-Dreyfusards were clearly drawn....For a large number the battle for Dreyfus had become a battle against the guardian institutions of traditional France—the Church and the Army—which seemed linked to the defense of the older France.[7]

As anti-Semitic incidents increased across France in what Bredin calls a "savage expression of collective anti-Semitism,"[8] Dreyfus, the man far removed from the cause fought by others, remained on Devil's Island, totally loyal to the army, never acknowledging that his religion might have had something to do with his treatment.

When the verdict came down in Rennes in September 1899, crowds in world capitals protested and private industry threatened to boycott the upcoming World's Fair in Paris. Although the French press was split, as was the public, between Dreyfusards and anti-Dreyfusards, most of the foreign press supported Dreyfus to the point where Austrian journalists claimed that the international press was surely in the hands of the Jews (after Zola's trial, the Austro-Hungarian press turned against France). When Dreyfus was retried in Rennes, *The New York Times* editorialized:

> In France...there are no rules of evidence....Witnesses have appeared before the Judges and have spoken their minds freely. They have not presented evidence....They have repeated conversations that they had heard at second or third hand....All this is called testimony in France.[9]

Coincidentally, it was in 1896 during the height of public furor over the Affair that *The New York Times* was purchased by the Ochs family, who were Jewish, and who would later intermarry with a family named Dryfoos.

It was clear that the trial was shaping up into a sensational event and the press was ready for it. Four hundred reporters were accredited to cover the trial. A wire room was set up so that the news could be flashed around the world instantly. Reporters were assigned desks and access to the telegraph machine to get their stories sent as soon as possible. There were six telegraph wires from Rennes to Paris, two wires to Brest where the French Cable company was located, and one wire to Havre where there was a connection with another company. There was only one clerk to help and what with the language differences and the large numbers of reporters, the difficulties were enormous. Reporters anxious to get their news out first, devised all kinds of strategies to rush their dispatches from the courtroom to the transmission center, a quarter mile away. On the first day, more than 650,000 words were transmitted.[10] Nothing like this kind of press operation had ever been seen before.

The reporting from Rennes was extraordinarily descriptive in evoking the excitement of the trial. For example, in depicting the appearance

of the handwriting expert on whom the first conviction had depended, the correspondent for the *London Times* writes, "Now and again M.
Bertillon's voice rose in hateful shrieks," and continues, "…in the Dreyfus
case…we are placed at the mercy of the fantastic mystifications of a dis-
ordered visionary's brain, for such Bertillon is, the Cagliostro of the 19th
century."[11] Describing the judges' attempts to understand the elaborate
system Bertillon developed and his convoluted explanations, the reporter's language is one of mockery and disbelief, "Today we have witnessed
the exposure of the incredible charlatanry of the unspeakable Bertillon."

An editorial appearing on August 15, 1899 in the *Herald Tribune* read:

> Doubtless many schemers who really care nothing about the Dreyfus case
> and would not lift a finger to save the rascals of the General Staff find in
> their danger and in their prejudice against the Jews an opportunity to make
> trouble![12]

The writer goes on to say that Frenchmen should awaken to the craze
of forgers and enemies of French liberty, especially after the attempt on
Labori's (one of Dreyfus' attorneys) life. No wonder there was such eager
readership for coverage of the trial!

The right wing paper published by Maurras and named after his organization, Action Française, never let up on the Dreyfus story from
the time the paper was founded in 1899. Quite remarkably, they managed to find story possibilities every day for years. Up to the outbreak of
World War I, when Maurras finally called a moratorium because of the
"common enemy," anti-Dreyfus columns were a regular feature of his
publication. The staying power of the issue of espionage and the correlation with anti-Jewish and anti-German feeling was incredible. For the
French press, the trial at Rennes and the subsequent pardon became the
primary story. No reader could escape hearing about it.

Even if one didn't read, the abundance of caricatures and cartoons were another avenue of information. Nancy Fitch, writing in the *American Historical Review*,[13] found in her research on the impact of the Affair in rural France that all kinds of powerful visual images were circulated; perhaps the most unusual were cigarette papers imprinted with Dreyfus' caricature. They were even called *bordereaux* and everyone knew what they represented. Fitch contends that even peasants were reading by the 1880s and that rumors and exaggerations acquired the force of truth. She studied in great detail an isolated rural area in southwest France where there were no Jews and found an atmosphere characterized by almost hysterical anti-Semitism.

Caricatures of Dreyfus were immediately recognizable abroad as well. Reaction was divided, but usually critical of France. Most Germans were convinced of Dreyfus' innocence. The trial was an occasion to reinforce the enmity Germany felt for France and to show to the world that Germany would not treat individual rights as lightly as its former enemy. The most respected paper in the German daily press, the *Frankfurter Zeitung*, was liberal and supported Dreyfus early on. The German government was not at all happy about the allegations of its complicity in the Affair.

The Germans also were of the opinion that anti-Semitism was far less strong in Germany than in France. Even some German Catholics believed in Dreyfus' innocence.[14] Between the German attitude and the general condemnation in Britain, it appeared that France had lost the respect of the civilized world. Some of the language condemning France is strong enough to make it appear that France should be isolated from the rest of Europe.

There were protests in many countries, with people asking their governments to boycott the 1900 World's Fair in Paris (L'Exposition.) Jewish groups in the United States and England expressed their anger at the verdict in a series of demonstrations. Well-known authors wrote criticizing the French abuse of individual rights. It seemed that every country in Europe had a point of view on the Affair, and most were critical of the way France had handled it. The division of opinion broke down fairly predictably along a demarcation line between Catholic and Protestant countries, but perhaps a better indicator of where they stood was the degree to which constitutionalism prevailed and to which dissent was tolerated.

Because of the government's preoccupation with ensuring the success of the World's Fair, the verdict against Dreyfus was very disturbing for its potential negative impact. Political leaders felt that favorable public opinion was crucial to the status of France as a respected world business power. The behind-the-scenes deal to pardon Dreyfus was negotiated quickly to put the matter out of the limelight, but once again the Affair refused to die. The press continued its vigilance when disagreement over the pardon made another good story.

Many in the Dreyfus camp felt that the pardon was a repudiation of the battle they had fought so hard. Clemenceau was especially outraged that the story should end without vindication; Picquart agreed with him. Thus, the story as reported in the world press continued to be an embarrassment. It seemed to have a life of its own and one which the media encouraged. Yet Kedward in his analysis says, "...only when Waldeck-Rousseau formed his ministry of republican solidarity and pardoned Dreyfus was control of events finally wrested from the editors and columnists."[15]

Unsurprisingly, much of the reporting of the time was biased. It was commonplace for newspapers to reflect their viewpoints in news stories, as well as in features and commentaries. The American press covered the story both in the major daily newspapers and in respected periodicals.

The story had captured the imagination of editors and received prominent placement on front pages and the editorial pages. The Chicago papers assigned special correspondents to write articles about Lazare and Clemenceau. Zola's articles were instrumental in awakening American writers to the case.

There was also coverage in the Yiddish language press and specialized Jewish publications. These served as links between the recent immigrants and pointedly reminded them of how fortunate they were to be out of Europe. Reading the papers of the time one is struck by the virtually unanimous condemnation of the French military. News articles vilified the French generals and evidently roused the American public. In Indiana, French flags were burned.

The American press, comparatively moderate in its coverage, nevertheless criticized France for its failure to observe democratic standards of justice. A columnist in *Harper's* magazine reporting on the trial at Rennes was shocked at how little affected the French people seemed to be, as they went about their daily business while "the most explosive trial of the century" was going on in their town. But his most severe criticism was leveled at the generals, who never admitted their mistake and continued to let Dreyfus suffer, wrongly accused.[16]

The Nation commented unequivocally that an Anglo-Saxon legal system would never have permitted the tortures endured by Dreyfus and that France was an example of a "de-civilized" state that had conducted a "ridiculous" trial. The notion of a fair trial, said the writer, has never gained a foothold in France, which was a nation captive to its military, and to an old-style militarism at that. It was the army that had led a civilized country down the wrong path. There was more than a whiff of Anglo-Saxon prejudice in these views.[17]

A thoughtful piece in the *Political Science Quarterly* by Frederick

Whitridge makes the argument that Americans know very little about foreign affairs and tend to accept what countries do at face value. He said because France calls itself a republic, Americans are misled and that the circumstances of Zola's trial and his sentencing should serve to alert people to the differences between our republic and the French. He compares M. Drumont, editor of *La Libre Parole*, to New York journalists on the Cuban question—all vitriol and little evidence. The comparison is apt. It is noteworthy that the Affair coincided with the "jingo" journalism of the contemporary Hearst papers in America.[18]

Whitridge furthers the implied comparison by saying that he cannot imagine that Dreyfus is living in a hut under the most cruel and inhumane conditions. "Every English speaking person finds it revolting that a man, however base, can, after a secret trial, be consigned to a living death on evidence he had no chance to answer." Whitridge proceeds "what impresses us is the immense caste and racial feeling, which segregates the army from the people and puts it above the law, and sets Jews almost outside the law."[19] This observation, though accurate, seems somewhat self-satisfied, implying that the United States is a paragon of republican virtue. It fails to take into account the condition of former slaves in the United States in the decades after the Civil War and the strong prejudices of the time against immigrants.

It is impossible to estimate French institutions by our own standards when France has no writ of habeas corpus, no grand jury, and no law of evidence as we understand it. He respects Zola for daring to say that the acquittal of Esterhazy was a criminal act, as was Dreyfus' court-martial. Whitridge concludes by speculating as to whether the French are entitled to use the term "republic" to describe their system of government. A piece in *The Spectator* makes the cases succinctly: "France is morally rotten and requires a new group of leaders."[20]

An article in the *Westminster Review*, after Dreyfus was freed, discusses the state of the French press in the period from the Franco-Prussian war to the time of the Dreyfus case. The author describes the press as a "total anarchy of utterance" where an irresponsible paper can print what it wants with no fear of prosecution. The anti-Dreyfusard press referred to the shooting in Rennes of Labori as a "joke." According to the author, malicious journalism has been the rule with little chance for sufficient redress. Much of the poison press was of Catholic origin, with *La Croix* cited as the "most abominable of all." [21] Strangely enough, *La Croix* acknowledged its maliciousness and issued an apology to the Jewish community—one hundred years after the case!

Overall, the coverage of the Affair in the American press was an opportunity for Americans to congratulate themselves on their system of justice. Although overwhelmingly in favor of Dreyfus and consistently portraying him as a victim, the newspapers and periodicals that published articles for the most part served an elite audience, unlike in France, where the Affair was extensively covered by the so-called penny press. Some of the worst excesses in "reporting" are found in those papers with mass readerships.

The American Jewish press of the era divides into English and Yiddish language. The English language readers had the *Jewish Daily News* and weeklies and monthlies such as the *Jewish Comment, Jewish Criterion, American Hebrew*, and the *American Jewess*. Perhaps responding to the dilemma of established Jewish leaders wary of seeming to place ethnic interests first, the press tried to describe the plight of Dreyfus in universal terms, rather than as a Jewish problem. The fears of the older Jewish community, consisting of people who were desperately trying to assimilate and who reacted with nervousness to the large waves of Eastern European immigrants, were understandable.

The Yiddish language press was more forthright than *The New York Times*, now owned by Jews, could afford to be. The power of Jewish-owned media was a rallying cry for anti-Semitism in the United States of the 20th century. Yet curiously and perversely, *The New York Times* has often been criticized by Jews for its lack of initiative on Jewish issues. It maintained an anti-Zionist posture for decades. Whether the subject has been domestic anti-Semitism, the Holocaust, or American policy toward Israel, the attitude and influence of *The New York Times* on these sensitive questions remains unresolved.

Newer Jewish immigrants to America than the German Jewish community were frightened by the potential for anti-Semitism in their adopted country and were concerned by the public discourse, as were the earlier immigrants. Yet, for those who were informed, the Affair provided a measure of commonality. When the Zionist Congress met in New York in 1899, they were delighted to receive a message of thanks from Lucie Dreyfus for their support of the cause. They felt the events of the Affair bolstered their argument for a Jewish state.

In 1906, when Dreyfus was formally vindicated and given a commission as a commandant in the army, *The New York Times* reported that although Dreyfus, now that he was again an officer, could not make statements for publication, he had conversations with friends in which he "did not conceal" his gratitude to the sympathetic treatment he received in the American press. He said it was a helpful influence in forming American sentiment and especially thanked *The New York Times* for its sensitive reporting.[22] The article reports that Dreyfus had not responded to his experience personally and had refused all offers of speaking tours. He wished to retain his privacy.

The British and the Germans seized on the Dreyfus story for different reasons and covered it to the hilt. England reveled in the opportunity to portray France as a nation which abused human rights. The British, always famous for letter writing, had much to say about the corruption of the French system and the abuse of rights. They said a lot of it in letters to the press, from the longest one ever run in *The Times* of London written by the Permanent Under Secretary of State for Home Affairs (see p. 129), to briefer, more inflamed missives from ordinary people. In general, the view was pro-Dreyfus and vehemently anti-French. Some of this anti-French sentiment was expressed by Lord Russell, who said what had happened was simply a lack of awareness on the part of the French that this was now an age of modern communications and they could not hide behind the screen of domestic concern. Nothing could be kept from the world at large in the age of the telegraph and the telephone.[23]

An article on British public opinion prepared by Nelly Wilson for the centennial symposium at Rennes emphasizes the fact that Britain was always home to failed French leaders, including royal pretenders. According to the author, the British were annoyed by many of these pretenders who tried to jump on the anti-Semitic bandwagon. There was little sympathy for their position. Moreover, for the British government, the question of whether the Third Republic was stable enough to maintain its overseas possessions was a crucial diplomatic issue.[24] As we know, Queen Victoria was an ardent supporter of the Dreyfusards. Zola, of course, chose to spend a year in exile in Great Britain.

Germany took particular pleasure in reporting the stonewalling reaction of the military to the exposure of the methods used in the original trial. The German interest was obviously connected to the still unclear role of the German military attaché, Schwarzkoppen, in the Affair and to a deep-seated contempt for the French military. There was also possibly a modicum of fear that this matter could trigger a serious incident between the two countries. After the publication of Zola's "J'Accuse," the German

Secretary of State, von Bulow, addressed the Reichstag to say that he denied categorically any contact between German officials and Dreyfus and that he knew nothing of the affair. Later, when Labori, Dreyfus' lawyer, sought the testimony of Schwartzkoppen, Kaiser Wilhelm rejected his request. The Kaiser would not publicly state he believed in Dreyfus' innocence, but kept to the story that Germany remained outside the affair in the hopes of not provoking any strong reaction from the French.

The German media, like most other media in Europe, divided along party lines, but unlike the French conservative press, the Germans were not entirely anti-Semitic in their reactions to Dreyfus. It is said that Germany in the late 19th century was far less anti-Semitic than neighboring Austria and France. To be a German nationalist did not necessarily equate with being an anti-Semite, nor did being a Catholic. Catholic opinion was not the lock-step adherence to the Church position that it was in France. German reporting frequently criticized the French for their weak government, mocking the Republic and praising their own constitutional monarchy. They often wrote that the Rights of Man, worshipped in the Revolution, no longer existed in France. Zola's "J'Accuse" had greater resonance for the liberal German press than the Dreyfus case itself.

Predictably, countries like Spain, much like Drumont in France, reiterated the vicious propaganda against the Jews issued by the Church. The foreign Catholic press continued to view the Dreyfus case through the prism of anti-Semitism and echoed the vitriol of the French papers. The writing repeated the calumnies of medieval times against Jews. Wholly preposterous charges against Dreyfus were reported as evidence. One read about Jewish conspirators, Christ-killers, people who would never find salvation, and other timeworn polemics that had little relevance to the Affair.

These stories reinforced and further enraged the public against the Jews, as though that were necessary in a country like Spain, which had gotten rid of its Jews four centuries before.

The Russians seemed to support France, but not in a way that would appeal to world opinion. The Russians did not understand what all the fuss was about. Had a similar case been before the military courts there, the action taken would have been swift and uncomplicated: "We would have sent him to Siberia or shot him without any publicity."[25]

Italy, as the seat of the Vatican was, of course, dominated by official Catholic opinion. In the years before the trial at Rennes, the pope had taken no action on the case, but most Italian newspapers thought that Dreyfus was guilty and that Zola was a pornographer. The Jesuit monthly, *Civilta Cattolica*, slandered Jews by saying they had been created by God to act as traitors.[26] Writing in an article for the Rennes symposium, Jean-Dominique Durand states that the pope had begun to worry about the Affair and by 1899 was convinced of Dreyfus' innocence.[27] He was upset by the vehement language of the Catholic press in France and Italy; nonetheless, he remained silent.

What was significant in the coverage was the extraordinary extent to which public opinion was mobilized, aroused, and informed. Many criticized the press for "trying" Dreyfus—an extremely modern criticism. By the time of the second court-martial at Rennes, the story was a familiar one to readers throughout Europe, the United States, and Latin America, a public spectacle observable by anyone interested enough to read a newspaper or a magazine. No wonder the French government was concerned about the nation's reputation and the success of the Paris World's Fair, with the pressure of public opinion a factor for the first time ever in a domestic trial.

For some critics, the French press had gone too far in reporting the Dreyfus Affair. G.W. Steevens, quoted in *Harper's*, concluded that public life had been harmed by the ferocity and sensationalism of the reportage. We might wonder about this assessment in light of the fact that the American press at the time was possessed by "jingo" fever. Steevens' writing is itself rather feverish. He says the French press had been "reckless" and the result was that "the degradation of politics and the army had been equalled by that of the press" which he goes on to say was totally discredited and "putrid." He offers an interesting comparison between two traumatic events. After the Revolution, there was great faith to galvanize in order to rebuild the nation. After the Dreyfus case, the great institutions still stood, but everybody knew them to be "rotten." [28]

A leading French intellectual and an assimilated Jew, Daniel Halévy, looked at the situation differently when, years after the Affair, he wrote about "the madness of public opinion" and asserted that it was the Dreyfus Affair that poisoned France and not the other way around.[29] It is difficult to perceive the logic of this view. He said that injustice has two victims—the one victimized and the other who inflicts injustice. It is a peculiar effort to justify a contrary position in the face of overwhelming evidence—a reflection of a man at odds with his own heritage.

When Dreyfus resumed military service as head of artillery in Vincennes and was a year later assigned to Paris, the story ended and his privacy was respected until World War I, when the retired commandant volunteered to serve his beloved France once more. Then there was a slight flurry of publicity, but it was hardly significant news. Dreyfus was no longer a page-one story. But, then, the story was never really about him anyway.

Eight

The Vichy Era

I have often felt... how difficult it was to speak of those
(occupation) days to anyone who had not lived through them....
Now, after nearly twenty years, I cannot recall the truth...
— *Simone de Beauvoir*, The Prime of Life

ALTHOUGH THE DREYFUS CASE was officially closed on July 12, 1906, when Dreyfus received word that the High Court had annulled the verdict of Rennes and reinstated his civil liberties, the Affair continued to be extremely significant in French politics. A French writer chose the following metaphor to describe the case: as a boat, and the Affair as the sea which exceeds it infinitely.[1]

When the case came to a conclusion, Dreyfus was able to live out his life in relative peace and tranquility with his family. But the inexorable movement of the sea could never be halted by a legal process and the Affair remained a key historic event, leaving its mark across two centuries of French culture. For Robert Hoffman, the author of *More Than a Trial*, the Affair lasted through Vichy.[2] That is an arguable understatement. From many perspectives, it is possible to say that the Affair still remains a force in France today.

Most evident is that the Affair foreshadowed the events of Vichy. The parallels are there: a revived anti-Semitism, a reactionary movement opposed to republican values, the attempted break with the revolutionary past, and a readiness to abandon republicanism in exchange for order and authority. These factors, combined with a strengthened relationship between the army and the Catholic church, are too obvious to ignore in any analysis of the Vichy era. It was as though seeds that had been buried for a half century began to germinate and push their way through the soil. For the Catholic church, the Vichy government provided the chance to restore what had been lost under the Third Republic. The cast of characters was different, but the roles remained virtually unchanged in the reprise of a century-old drama, was now set in Vichy. Reactionary values held center stage.

With the outbreak of World War I, just a brief generation removed from the Affair, the Dreyfus family showed its patriotism by serving in the French military once more. Pierre Dreyfus, Alfred's son, had a particularly splendid combat record and earned the Croix de Guerre. His sister's husband worked as a surgeon on the battlefields. As we know, Dreyfus himself was mobilized at his request in the summer of 1914. Michael Burns talks of the irony of alliances between former enemies in the interest of patriotism. Anti-Dreyfusards joined with Dreyfusards in gestures of solidarity and toasted their country before going off to war.[3] The Dreyfus extended family of nephews and cousins suffered many losses in the Great War, as did most French families in the four years of bloody combat.

Yet these sacrifices for their country would not count for much in the Second World War. Marshal Pétain's announced goal was to preserve in the Vichy government the old values of France. The position taken by this doddering old man is a surreal reverberation of the Dreyfus Affair. Pétain's commander-in-chief, General Maxime Weygand, said that France needed to get rid of the old order of things, which was a "political regime of Masonic, capitalist...and international...compromises." This was decades after Weygand had helped finance the anti-Semitic movement for Lieutenant Colonel Henry's defense and who, in his seventy-third year, still firmly believed in Alfred Dreyfus's guilt....[4] For those who sympathized with Weygand, Pétain's insistence on traditional values gave them the opportunity to emphasize their belief that the Jews by their very existence undermined those values. The Vichy regime soon replaced the revolutionary slogan of *Liberté, Égalité, Fraternité* with *Travail, Famille, Patrie*. This, in essence, expressed the "race policy" of the Vichy administration. It was both a contrarian family values statement and a negation of the democratization promulgated by the Revolution.

Toward the end of the 20th century, there was an exhibit on Vichy at Les Invalides in Paris, complete with videos containing the sights and sounds of Pétain's triumphal processions through French villages. The enthusiasm of his welcome, usually by little blonde girls bearing huge bouquets of flowers, was reminiscent of the welcomes received by Soviet officials in the most repressive years of their regime. It was difficult to connect the frightening rhetoric of Laval and other Vichy officials with the glowing, innocent faces on the screen.

One of the factors contributing to the resurgence of anti-Semitism in France in the 1930s, along with the effects of a global depression of major proportions, was the high rate of immigration, much of it illegal and thus difficult to tabulate. Because of the losses of men in World War I, France actively sought foreign workers for its industry and agriculture in the 1920s. Although many of these workers returned to their countries in the early 30s when the depression began to hit France, there was a simultaneous influx of refugees from eastern Europe, to the point where France had a higher proportion of foreigners than any other industrialized country. Ordinary Frenchmen were concerned about the influx when the depression took hold and unemployment soared. A pervasive xenophobia dominated the outlook of many French workers between the wars. Other people became obsessed with the threat to French culture posed by so many foreigners. Many of them were Jews fleeing Hitler and their presence rekindled deep-rooted prejudices, along with fears of unemployment and international conspiracies.

Marrus and Paxton, who have written authoritatively on the subject, make the point that this surge of anti-Semitism between the wars was not confined to a small, right-wing group. Many leading intellectuals felt it was necessary to preserve French values, as Pétain often stated. The playwright, Jean Giraudoux, for example, wanted a "ministry of race." He believed that Ashkenazi Jews were by definition "contrary to the French artisan spirit of precision, trust, perfection." [5]

"But there was a Jewish problem before the war! The Jews had gone too far." [6] This is what the son of a Vichy minister said to Adam Nossiter, author of *The Algeria Hotel*, during an interview many decades later. It makes it easier to understand how the Pétain government in 1941 could have instituted a Commissariat for Jewish Affairs to implement the scores of anti-Jewish measures that Vichy had passed since October 1940, with no prompting from Germany. [7]

Additionally, when Germany demanded that all French Jews pay a fine totaling one billion francs, Jewish bank accounts were raided, including that of Dreyfus' widow. There seemed to be no brakes on the extreme actions of the Vichy officials, which were driven by blatant race hatred. So much for protection of French citizens and the near reverence for citizenship born during the Revolution. It was clearly an outright policy of state anti-Semitism. According to Burns, referring to Vichy, "Anti-semitism has recovered its inevitable force." [8]

The anti-Jewish statutes of the Vichy regime compared "favorably" to those of the Nazis in their emphasis on racial purity. These laws, known as the Alibert laws, defined "Jew" as anyone having more than two grandparents of the Jewish "race." Gradually Jews began to lose their freedom and their status. They were excluded from professions connected to journalism and entertainment and were strictly limited in other fields. The laws were enforced by the General Commission for Jewish Questions. Pierre Laval, Pétain's vice-premier, was key to the severity of the enforcement. He sent a directive to his office in 1942 that Jews should not be referred to as "Mr. Levy" or "Mr. Dreyfus," but as "the Jew Levy" and "the Jew Dreyfus;" the latter is a revealing choice of a proper name. [9]

A few months later, Laval ordered that children be included in the deportation order of families from the unoccupied zone; he was not at all concerned with the fate of the children. This was recorded by a Nazi official in a report. Laval's commitment to fascism went quite far; he had no faith in parliamentary government and wished for an authoritarian regime.

Pétain dismissed him in December 1940 and he spent the next two years with the Nazi occupiers in Paris, until he was called back to a virtually powerless Vichy in 1942 and worked for the Germans, carrying out their deportations and slave labor policies. Another Nazi official wrote in February of 1943 that Laval was willing to approve any anti-Semitic measures in exchange for political gain. He thought his unrelenting hunting down of Jews would mean a lessening of the constant German demands for food and French labor that were weakening the economy. [10] There is no evidence to support this belief.

Since the end of World War II, the French collaboration with the Nazis has been re-examined and found not to be one of frightened passivity, but of active cooperation and frequent initiative on anti-Jewish measures. The same word, *vendus* (sellouts), that was used to describe collaborators in the Vichy era had been used by Dreyfusards 50 years earlier. As Robert O. Paxton writes in his book on Vichy France, the anti-Semitic legislation passed by Vichy was entirely French—including the seizing of Jewish property and the deportation of the Jews. The Germans had little interest in Vichy policies, as long as there was stability in the society. [11]

Michael Marrus, co-author of *Vichy France and the Jews*, says that France was unique in its indigenous anti-Semitic policies, going beyond German expectations. [12] The bureaucracy proved extremely efficient in responding to the Nazi goal of getting rid of the Jews. In his book on the operations of the Vichy government, Adam Nossiter labels the actions of bureaucrats as "meticulous" in purging Jews from all professions and universities, taking a detailed census of Jews for use by the police and divesting them of their property. [13]

Only one other country voluntarily rounded up and handed over Jews outside the area of German occupation and that was Bulgaria, in the contested region of Macedonia. Other historians agree with Marrus' assessment of French actions. For example, Philippe Burrin, in his book, *France Under the Germans*, argues that the Vichy leadership used "the defeat as an opportunity to change the country's institutions, instead of making the survival of the nation its priority." [14] It was a chance to reshape France along anti-republican lines and recover a lost nation. The Germans were able to exploit this ideological position for their own purposes.

Perhaps the person who best exemplifies the nature of the French collaboration with the Nazis is Maurice Papon, the very model of a French civil servant. Convicted and sentenced to ten years in prison by a court in 1998 after an investigation that lasted sixteen years, Papon had been subject to 764 charges brought by prosecutors in connection with his role in the deportation of Jews from Bordeaux, where he was prefect.

Papon embodies Hannah Arendt's theory of Nazi bureaucrats who represent the "banality of evil."[15] His history as a civil servant is remarkable. He began as a young radical socialist in the 30s, served Vichy in the 40s, and amazingly was part of the Gaullist regime in the next decades. At one point, he held the position of chief of police in Paris and headed up the special force responsible for killing hundreds of rioting Algerians in Paris in 1961.

The Commissioner-General for Jewish Affairs, Xavier Vallat, notorious for his implacable anti-Semitic views, was tried after the war and said in his defense that anti-Semitism was good because it prevented a minority group from influencing a Christian country.[16] Admittedly, the French had a much greater refugee problem than other countries because the Germans had dumped Jews from the East into France, but the French even turned their own Jewish citizens into virtual refugees by depriving them of the right to earn a living and by stamping their identity cards with a large "J" for Juif. In so doing, the government effectively condemned them to starvation. At the same time, the Germans had shipped many Frenchmen to work in Germany for the war effort. As a result, the French economy plummeted to the point where there were severe food shortages and malnutrition was prevalent in many areas.

The data on the deportation of Jews, including children, have been exhumed from historical records and were used in the Klaus Barbie trial more than 40 years after the fact. Of the 4,051 children rounded up for deportation in the notorious *grand rafle*, not one survived. When the leader of the French Protestant Church complained to Pétain about the deportation of children, he was granted a meeting with Laval, who told him all Jews would be hunted down regardless of age. Both the Protestant and the Catholic churches in France tried to save Jewish children at their own peril, often hiding them in convents or schools. However, these horrifying roundups of Jews were made possible by a census that the Vichy government obligingly took for the Germans.

According to Milton Dank, the ties between the Church and Vichy began to loosen when it became known the French were being sent to forced labor camps and the Jews were being deported to death camps.[17] However, Pétain—although, like most of his compatriots, only a nominal Catholic—had become totally identified with the most right wing elements of the Church, and all state schools were clericalized in his regime. This supports the theory that the French government acted not as a puppet under orders from the Vatican, but in what it perceived to be its own interests. Returning the curricula of French schools to Catholic indoctrination, anathema since the Revolution, was a Vichy initiative and did not originate with the Vatican.

In the reaction of the French church and its connection with Vichy, there are implicit questions about the influence of the Vatican. Where was the leader of world Catholicism in this trying time? What did the Pope say or do to alleviate the persecution and suffering of millions? How did he influence his French adherents? What were his relations with the Vichy government? Many of these questions have been subjects of research by both Catholic and non-Catholic writers.

Ironically, many similar questions were also raised in connection with Dreyfus' case. In an emotional article in *Commonweal*, an American Catholic publication, Kathleen McCaffrey writes that "Although religion itself was not a theme at the Barbie trial... crimes against humanity cannot be separated from the concerns of religion, and of the Catholic

Church."[18] The Vatican has explained its policy in later years as "quiet diplomacy," but the picture that emerges from scholarly research does not accord with this view of the Vatican's inaction.

The notion of German guilt for what happened in France was advanced and found wanting by a later generation of Frenchmen, who asked their fathers and grandfathers to take responsibility. History is being rewritten as the present generation looks at the evidence of prejudice and betrayal. Ironically, a shameful period of French history has been the impetus for a spate of excellent films, starting with Ophuls' *The Sorrow and the Pity*, an unrelenting depiction of how people acted in a time of crisis. Later films continue the cinematic tradition of unsparing looks at human behavior under pressure. There was no need to fictionalize the actions, which speak for themselves.

A surprising fact is that, despite anti-Semitism, Jewish writers and artists have always felt at home in France, more so than in other European countries. This was certainly true of upper-middle class Jews. Even Dreyfus' son, Pierre, like his father, was blind to the French race hatred and put his trust in the Vichy government, at least through its first year. Léon Blum and other prominent Jews also initially trusted the Pétain regime, only to have that trust betrayed and their lives imperiled.

Like many of their co-religionists in other countries, French Jews had assimilated into the society where they were residing and had always considered themselves good citizens. Their reaction to Vichy policies was one of surprise and shock. It seemed impossible that Léon Blum, along with the former prime minister Édouard Daladier, would be sent to prison and then to concentration camps.

The prevalent trust in assimilationism which had characterized the established French Jewish community was completely shattered during Vichy, as they were forced to wear the same yellow "J" as their immigrant co-religionists. Denial of a long history of anti-Semitism was no longer a credible reaction. Whether or not some Jews were ambivalent about being Jewish, the Vichy policy makers were not. A Jew was a Jew, no matter his origin or his length of residence in France.

Paxton writes of the moral complicity of the Vichy leadership in their initiatives against the Jews and their approval of Nazi policies. Pétain, who was revered by the French masses, used his position to rubber-stamp the most racist German acts and refused to protect the Jews who sought asylum in the Unoccupied Zone. [19] Other European countries, Denmark in particular, arranged for the escape of Jews to safety, but Vichy provided no such assistance. Obsessed with saving France, Pétain did not admit to the inhumanity of Vichy refugee policies. In the end, of course, silence equals complicity when lives are at stake; that is crucial.

George Steiner, the well-known British literary critic, himself a refugee from the horrors of occupied France, has no trouble assessing blame when he expresses a view on the comparative evil of French and German anti-Semitism, that, though extremely harsh, has a basis in fact. He had said that all France lacked was a Hitler to lead the people and the horrors perpetrated by the Nazis would have taken place in France. From his perspective, had French leadership been more dynamic, the equivalent of Nazism would have occurred in France. [20]

Why this dichotomy in France between cosmopolitanism and intense chauvinism should exist is difficult to fathom. Some have said it can be explained by the openness to change and creativity in Paris, as compared to the closed society of traditional France—a clear urban/rural split in values. Yet it was in Paris that thousands of Jews were arrested, detained, and led to their deaths with the help of cooperative neighbors. The Vélodrome in the city was a holding area for Jews before they embarked on the final journey to Auschwitz; the notorious detention center of Drancy is located only three miles outside Paris. There is now a plaque commemorating the deportation of the Jews to the Nazi concentration camps over a period of three years. Only in 2001 was it decided to honor as a historic monument the place where so many Jews were detained.

An article in *Le Monde* refers to Drancy as the antechamber of Auschwitz. Under the leadership of a young mayor, Drancy has recently won historic preservation status. The mayor remarked that no elected official had ever come to Drancy as an act of remembrance.[21] One hundred thousand people were shipped out; most of them died in the East. Despite the fact that it was Hitler's personnel who engineered the deportation, it was left to the French police to administer Drancy and to load the trains to the death camps. Nearly 60 years later, Holocaust survivors and their heirs have brought suit against the French national railroad for running these death trains for the Nazis.[22]

Lucie Dreyfus managed to leave Paris when the Germans came. Her brave exodus was quietly dramatic. Despite her age, she set out on an arduous trek through southern France; her remarkable journey is one of survival and faith. Almost 50 years earlier, she had steadfastly supported her husband's cause, raised two young children, and had written daily to Dreyfus in exile. Now, along with thousands of other Parisian Jews, she would lose her home and her possessions, and herself be forced into an exile filled with hardships. Her story of survival is extraordinary. She was sheltered for a period of time by nuns in a convent in Valence, where this upper-middle class woman did needlework to earn her keep. A woman in her seventies, she was strong enough physically and morally to support herself. She traveled regularly through the unoccupied zone to maintain contact with her widely dispersed extended family.

When it became clear that the Vichy government was not going to shield its Jewish population, whether or not they were citizens, several younger members of the Dreyfus family joined the Resistance. Madeleine Lévy was one of those resistance fighters; she was Lucie's favorite granddaughter and died at the hands of the Nazis in Auschwitz, much as the previous generation of the Dreyfus family had given their lives to their country in World War I. The stalwart Mme. Dreyfus outlived her husband by 10 years, dying in Paris in 1945 of natural causes, exacerbated by the difficult circumstances of the last years of her life.

In the immediate postwar period, important questions were not asked in public. Should France feel guilty for its actions in World War II? Did its willing collaboration with the Nazis send Jews to their deaths who might otherwise have been saved? Did they, by refusing help and protection to refugees, permanently blot their moral copybook? How much had the environment changed since the frame-up of a Jewish officer in 1894 unleashed a firestorm of protest from other democratic nations?

If justice is ultimately served, then the sentencing of Charles Maurras, the anti-Semitic writer-philosopher who headed Action Française, is a good example. His organization, founded in 1899, endured to become a leading exponent of the ideology of the Vichy government. It had never accepted republican ideals, but was organized to re-create the "old France" before it was corrupted by the ideas of liberty and equality. Maurras was a fanatic admirer of Pétain, whom he regarded as something of a national savior. In a chilling instance of supreme irony, Maurras was put to death in 1945 for aiding the Germans against the French—the same sentence he had passionately advocated for Dreyfus, fifty years before.

The trial of Pétain in July and August 1945 was an historic event and revealed much of the thinking of the Vichy government by what was said and unsaid. Pétain, at the age of eighty-nine, delivered an opening statement absolving himself of responsibility and asserting that he had given his life as a "gift" to France. A parade of Vichy officials took the stand and almost unanimously denied culpability for what the government had done to its citizens—in testimony eerily reminiscent of the generals who testified in the Dreyfus case, convinced of the correctness of their actions. Laval particularly was contemptuous of the entire proceedings. The public seemed divided between admiration for a man who was once synonymous with French glory and disgust for a man who had acted ignominiously in the face of an occupying force.

In 1987, when Klaus Barbie, a German, was brought from Latin America to be judged for war crimes during the Vichy regime, the nervous attitude of the French public revealed how close to the surface were the fears of exposure of atrocities committed by French officials during World War II. The nation was confronted with a state-sanctioned policy directed against part of its population. The coverup and lies of the Army during the Dreyfus Affair pale in comparison. Had this issue not yet been resolved in French society? Was Barbie, in the docket, just an old, tired man who should be left to live out his life in tranquility, or was he truly the "Butcher of Lyon"? Who should pay for his misdeeds? Was he simply another Eichmann, an automaton following orders? But whose orders? After all, Barbie was not acting for the French rulers, but the Nazi SS command. And why were these genocidal orders ever a part of Vichy policy?

It is easy to point the finger at the Vichy government, as with other governments in countries overrun by the Nazis, particularly since the French had a degree of autonomy that was absent in other countries subject to Nazi rule. The deal Pétain struck with the Nazis did give autonomy to his government in the unoccupied zone. The question of whether his was a puppet government or a sovereign one must be considered in determining responsibility and accountability. Germany placed different pressures on the countries it invaded, depending on its strategic goals;

for example, France had initially been used as a destination for refugees fleeing the east. In defense of many of those tried as war criminals after the Liberation, lawyers argued that although they may have gotten their hands dirty, they had no idea of the true nature of the Nazi "final solution." They could not have known that they were sending Jews to certain death. Although reports had been filed by diplomats and journalists in other countries about the massacre of 700,000 Polish Jews,[23] many could not believe these reports were true.

Even the Allies had trouble accepting the legitimacy of the stories of atrocities and medical experiments they were hearing. Therefore, they had to be wild exaggerations. Whatever their perceptions, the Vichy leaders resisted all appeals from French Jews to end the roundups and deportations. In the summer of 1942, these deportations reached a high point, so that it was no longer possible to rationalize them away; by the end of 1942, 42,000 Jews had been sent from France to Auschwitz.[24]

> It was the public roundups in the Unoccupied Zone on 26–28 August that swept away many hesitations. French police were seizing Jews on Marshal Pétain's doorstep and delivering them to the Germans; the complicity of the Vichy regime could no longer be veiled.[25]

Marrus and Paxton point out that there was a kind of backlash in France against foreigners—shades of the Dreyfus case. In the period between the wars, there had been an influx of aliens from central Europe in the 1930s—more than any other European country—and, although it denied them citizenship, France did help them economically. This was certainly better than the record of the United States and Canada. The authors see an explanation in this for what they call a "general loss of tolerance for foreigners and a more specific antisemitism of the 1940s." They also say that the Vichy government at the outset had more support than the "between the wars" regimes in France and needed that popular support to stay in power. They capitalized on the public's dislike of foreigners and the fact that Jews, again as in Dreyfus' time, were easily blamed for the economic privations suffered by ordinary Frenchmen.[26]

Yet, it is the contention of the authors that France played into German hands by putting up so little resistance. In some other countries, like Italy, those in power simply refused to act on the German orders for elimination of the Jews. This despite the fact the Vatican never publicly expressed any disagreement or disapproval of the anti-Semitic measures taken by Vichy. Marrus and Paxton assert that "France was altogether unique among occupied Western European nations in having adopted indigenous antisemitic policies...that (the French) were more like Rumania and Hungary than Spain and Portugal who were Hitler's allies."[27] Even a fascist country like Spain did not assist in sending Jews to their deaths. In Finland, which resisted the deportation policy and where no Jews were deported, Germany showed it could accept limits to its authority. In their anxiousness to please the Germans, the French never tested these limits.

Although they acknowledge the efforts of private individuals to save and shelter the Jews, the authors conclude that if the French police had not taken even small measures, like identifying and rounding up Jews as efficiently as they did, the Germans would have been seriously hampered in their goal of annihilation of the Jews. The French may not have participated in the killings, but they smoothed the way for the Nazis to do so, by providing the bureaucratic apparatus for tracking down Jews. Many critics feel they did the least of any country to protect their Jewish population. Their hands were not clean. In effect, they provided legitimacy for the actions of their occupiers.

It took years after the war was over for people to acknowledge the extent of the collaboration of the French with the Nazis. The few Jewish survivors who returned from the death camps and told their stories were treated as an embarrassment to the French people, much as Vietnam veterans were in the United States for other reasons.

From an historical perspective, it is possible to recognize in the actions of the Vichy government strong parallels to the Dreyfus Affair. First, we see pure racism in the indifference to the pain inflicted on a group of individuals, who have long been regarded as different and as handy whipping boys. Second, the deeply ingrained anti-foreign attitudes in France overriding the humanity of individuals toward one another. Third, since their resentment and sense of humiliation at the hands of the Germans were impossible to act on, both the preceding reasons fit nicely together in an attempt to regain lost esteem by a defeated nation.

What is surprising is that, unlike the Dreyfus coverage, which was extensive and prominently featured in the newspapers and journals of the time, the trials of Barbie and other Vichy officials failed to attract the same kind of worldwide attention. Relegated to the inside pages with the news from France, the trial was reported in major newspapers, but it was certainly possible for the reader or viewer of the daily American media to miss the story. The same holds true for the Le Pens, who are covered today as a domestic phenomenon.

The Dreyfus Affair opened the door to human rights concerns and gave the press an opportunity to deal with a new type of story. Perhaps the Nazi era, with all its atrocities, numbed editors to the nature of the crimes. Or perhaps the fact that the events were more than 40 years in the past limited the impact of the story and controlled news judgment. It might be too much to expect that reportage would demonstrate an understanding of fascism.

Furthermore, the bar has been raised today on what kinds of stories have staying power, with the huge number of newsworthy events competing for attention. Understandably, the public has grown more fickle and less attentive as a result of the flood of information presented each day in print and electronic journalism.

David Lewis sets forth the argument about the complicity of the Vichy government concisely:

> The anti-Semitism which was both cause and consequence of the Affair had found ultimate and terrible expression in German National Socialism and in the Fascism of Marshal Phillipe Pétain's État Français.[28]

One of the clearest manifestations of Nazism was to be found in Pierre Laval, whose person and actions made him a willing agent of the Germans. He believed that parliamentary democracy "lost the war" and would of necessity disappear and an authoritarian regime would replace it. Of course, the roots of fascism are present in every nation when people look for leadership and security. In bad times, fascism often seems to be a solution. Anti-republican sentiment goes back a long way in France and Laval linked it with a tradition of "grandeur," which was in danger of disappearing.

For the majority of Frenchmen, Pétain, with his wartime associations and his venerable age, represented the security of a father figure. The respect for Pétain approached cult status, as we have seen in the films of the Vichy era in which Pétain receives tearful emotional greetings as he makes his ceremonial entry into towns and villages. He seems a benign Hitler, responding to the cheers and bouquets of the crowds.

When Pétain and Maurras met during the Occupation, they congratulated each other on their dedication to "honor" amidst the foreign threats to their nation. Maurras had never wavered in his hatred of foreigners. For him the environment of Vichy France was comfortable, coinciding with his prejudices, much as the Dreyfus Affair had been a perfect setting for his beliefs. Fascism had had a strong appeal in France since the Third Republic and the old commander had enough political sense in his declining years to capitalize on it. As far back as the period between the wars the important fascist party, the Parti Populaire Français, had organized and developed a following. Milton Dank reports that racism was key to the growth of the party, which eventually broke up but was revived during the Occupation. The old refrains of the sanctity of the nation and the need for obedience to the state were not restricted to Germany. In his latter days, Maurras even referred to Pétain as a *führer*. The parallels are clear.

What seemed to be at stake during Vichy was a fundamental value system. Who was to define the French nation? Who were the truly French? It seemed like a replication of the divisions between the revolutionaries and the counter-revolutionaries of the 19th century. The battle of values continued to be fought between democratic and anti-democratic forces.

For a majority, it was the old war hero, Maréchal Pétain, who best represented France, a symbol both of traditional military glory and of strength of the family. Of course, this was a superficial perception based on his past reputation and his physical image. Pétain, for all his emphasis on family, was well-known as a man with an eye for the ladies, right up to and including the time of his trial. Furthermore, he was a man who by no means could be described as a practicing Catholic. Yet in the minds of his loyal supporters, he fit the image of France they wanted to project to the world.

If history can be understood through Herodotus' metaphor of a flowing river, constantly changing form, then what endures unchanging in the history of the Dreyfus Affair and the Vichy regime are the well-worn stones in the historic river of French anti-Semitism. The resurgence of anti-Semitism in the period between the wars accelerated with the defeat of 1940, much as the defeat in the Franco-Prussian War intensified anti-Semitic feelings. It can not be easily explained as a reaction to economic hard times, but has a deeper psychological basis. One cannot truly say that the Dreyfus Affair ended with Vichy, because we see in present-day France the manifestations of racism and nationalism that have marked French history in the 20th century.

In the same way that slavery ended in the United States, but racism persists, such was the end of the Dreyfus Affair. It has left in its wake an unsavory legacy. J. Hampden Jackson perceptively articulated the thought in his biography of Jean Jaurès:

> The Dreyfus affair was in very truth a dress rehearsal for the coming century; Germany was already a bogey in the wings, Russia a sinister deus ex machina and Paris, as was proper, the scene of the conflict of the ideologies. [29]

The 20th century would be the setting for other disreputable political scenarios in which France did not play a heroic role.

Nine

The Aftermath of the Affair
Unfinished Business

When will foreigners living in France have to wear a star?
—Bernard Stassi, centrist political leader (1991)

THE PASSAGE OF TIME has not eliminated the problem of anti-Semitism in France. After a period of quiet following the Vichy era, the next generation of French began to explore the uncomfortable question in an attempt to come to terms with their history. Because the Germans had been the condemned wrongdoers, attention was focused on their guilt in the post-war years, while the French managed to remain in the background on the issue. They were able to do this largely because of the popular, worldwide perception of France, which was concentrated on the person of Charles de Gaulle as a World War II ally. By the 1970s, however, a reassessment of France under the Germans began with an outpouring of literature and film on the French-Jewish experience, much of it produced by those who were children during the war years.

These artistic works became controversial because they awakened memories of shameful actions many would have preferred to forget. One of the most significant films, *The Sorrow and the Pity*, a documentary made by Marcel Ophuls in 1971, was not even shown on television in France until the newly elected Mitterand government lifted its embargo in 1981, thus enabling a much wider audience for the film. It dealt with the inhumanity of ordinary people toward each other in times of stress. It opened old wounds and shocked audiences in countries where the film was distributed, who had not paid much attention to the role of the French in the mass deportations and subsequent extermination of the Jews.

Following that film there was a veritable deluge of powerful autobiographical films about the experience of Jewish children in wartime France, few of which reflected particularly well on the country. Viewing these films, moviegoers all over the world received for the first time a different and disturbing perspective on the French from the one widely circulated and accepted during the war. For many Americans, it was a harsh eye-opener into the mentality of a country and culture much admired by intellectuals. The Affair changed the image of France as a "civilized" country. For most of the French, the question of collective guilt raised by the films and the reality of the trials of the Vichy executioners was a subject they would have preferred not to address, but one they could no longer avoid.

Then, in 1987, the well-publicized trial of Klaus Barbie forced a reconsideration of the relatively benign picture that prevailed in the popular mind of the French role, vis-à-vis the Nazis, in the war. Almost 100 years after the Dreyfus trial, a nation was asked to confront anti-Semitism as a human rights issue. Although one man was on trial for crimes against humanity, the reality was one man carrying out a state-approved policy, with the emphasis on the state. The Eichmann trial had made this an immediately understandable way of looking at the situation. The context was that of criminal activity directed against a particular group of people, which had escalated to a universal crime. A century after Dreyfus and 43 years after the end of the Vichy regime, it was France on trial.

The case against Barbie was serious enough to hire the Klarsfelds, well-known Nazi hunters, to track down the man who had fled to South America and to bring him back for trial. By the 21st century, this type of operation would become common practice. Whether this was a desire for vengeance or for closure, it was of importance to the French to confront the Vichy experience in a personal way. While the hunt for Barbie was in progress, he was tried and convicted in absentia and received the death sentence. Forgetting was no longer an option for the French.

In a sober article in *The New Yorker*,[1] Jane Kramer describes the Barbie trial as a sort of purgation for the French, who had lived through four humiliating years under Vichy—another haunting parallel with the Dreyfus era and the shame of defeat in the Franco-Prussian war. Although Barbie was now an old man and most of his peers were dead, it was a necessary exercise for the French in terms of their history, to "settle the score," as Kramer puts it.

After four years and 23,000 pages of testimony and instruction, Klaus Barbie was convicted of crimes against humanity committed 43 years before. Barbie was arrested in Bolivia in 1983 and extradited to France. He had already been tried twice in absentia and sentenced to death twice for war crimes. Since those trials, France had abolished the death penalty. In a supreme instance of irony, the man who then held the position of Justice Minister, Robert Badinter, was the son of a man who had been deported to Auschwitz by Barbie.

In his client's defense, Barbie's lawyer tried to come up with crimes against humanity committed by the Resistance, by the French army in

Algeria, and anything else he could find. Despite these efforts to equate other crimes with those of his client, Barbie was tried on 341 specific counts and found guilty by nine jurors, then sentenced to life imprisonment by three judges. Barbie didn't show up after the third day of the trial—claiming he was not in France and that he had been illegally extradited. "He had neither conscience, nor remorse." [2] Journalists lost interest; they had been expecting courtroom theater and now the principal actor was not there to play his role in the drama.

Once again, echoes of the Dreyfus case reverberated. For many who knew their history, the ghost of Dreyfus hovered over the proceedings. In the aftermath of the trial, violence against Jews broke out in Paris and in regions sympathetic to Le Pen (Klaus Barbie died in prison in 1991).

Kramer discusses what she terms a particular vogue for history in France comparable to the history of the turn of the century. She sees in the trials of Vichy officials a response to France's performance during the four years of the Occupation. The more recent trial of Maurice Papon raised questions similar to those of the Barbie case and provided another opportunity for expiation and a renewed interest in World War II history—and, as many have suggested, ended a period of deliberate amnesia.

When Papon was extradited from Switzerland, the French news media covered the story thoroughly. To the surprise of many observers (and apparently to Papon as well), Switzerland did not fall back on its famed neutrality to shield him. Nonetheless, many French felt Papon's illustrious career as a civil servant, along with his age should spare him punishment. After 16 years of investigation, the French leaders knew very well what his record was and how ably he had deflected attention from this record, continuing with his career through several changes in government. The underlying questions about duty to the state and personal morality remained unsettled. Despite the hundreds of charges against him, the court absolved him from knowingly participating in a systematic plan for the elimination of the Jews.

Also, as the century drew to a close, we had the interesting case of the Chilean dictator, General Augusto Pinochet, notorious for his abuse of human rights. Old and ailing in England, geography did not save him from extradition to his home country when Spain, of all nations, sought his extradition to stand trial for crimes against humanity. The president of Chile at the time was quoted in *The New York Times* as saying that "globalization has now expanded from economic affairs to the institutions of politics and justice." [3] One hundred years before, when Dreyfus was in exile on Devil's Island, the press was unable to continue its coverage of the story by following him to his place of imprisonment.

Imagine, a hundred years after Captain Dreyfus was deprived of his civil rights and finally released after world pressure, we have human rights organizations pressing for justice in all parts of the world. Unfortunately, similar to the French experience with Barbie and Papon, as the degree of horror has escalated, the public response seems to have diminished.

A more recent case involved a Mexican public official, an Argentinian by birth, who ran an infamous torture machine in Argentina during the Dirty War. Mexico granted a request to extradite Ricardo Cavallo from Spain, many of whose citizens "disappeared" in Argentina. The Spanish government wanted Mr. Cavallo to stand trial in their courts on charges of torture and crimes against humanity.

The parallels with the Dreyfus Affair are many and perhaps even more pointed because of the increase in the attentiveness of the public that has accompanied the vast changes in communications since the turn of the century. More people are aware of the events in other countries and human rights have become a universal concern. Of course, the United Nations Declaration of Human Rights provides a statement of intent to support and protect these rights. There are now international courts that establish procedures for determining and judging such crimes. The United Nations intends to create a new international criminal court, but so far the United States position is that it would be a violation of national sovereignty. A regional economic organization like the European Union has in its charter a standard of human rights. Naturally, a declaration does not solve an age-old problem of anti-Semitism or genocide practiced by custom or fiat. Whereas once this might have been considered an infringement on the autonomy of domestic politics, it is now widely, although not totally, accepted.

The way Kramer assesses the new preoccupation with the Vichy regime is: "History in France has always had a pedagogic function. It is 'true' insofar as it is useful in serving an idea of France." The French want a past that confirms "a kind of collective emotional identity." Calling up Occupation memories foils this goal. Evidence for this view was provided by those on the margin of the Barbie debate, a group of anti-Semitic historians, who sought to establish a revisionist interpretation of the Holocaust by labeling it self-serving Zionist propaganda. Interestingly enough "…the original revisionists were Dreyfusards. The word was used for people like Émile Zola, who wanted to 'revise' the judgment" on Dreyfus.[4] Now, revisionism has been appropriated by French neo-Nazis to support their view of the Vichy years. During the Barbie trial, they attempted to find academic supporters and arguments to disprove the Holocaust.

Although there is no clarity on what constitutes a crime against humanity, "France was the first—and is still the only—country in Europe to take the concept of 'crime against humanity' as it was written into the Nuremberg statutes, and give it a binding legal definition within its own penal code."[5] Time and place do not matter for crimes against humanity—they are committed everywhere and forever. There is no statute of limitations.

The Action Française of Dreyfus' time has been replaced by the far-right-wing Front National (FN) of Jean-Marie Le Pen. Two months after Barbie was sentenced, Le Pen went on the radio and said that Hitler's gas chambers were a "minor detail" in the history of the Second World War.[6] Yet the fascist elements of French society were less overtly anti-Semitic than they had been a century before. Racism was still a major factor in Le Pen's appeal, but it was focused more on immigrants, especially North Africans, than on Jews. Le Pen was successful in organizing a party to publicize his platform of "France for the French,"[7] and field candidates at the local and national level. The question reiterated endlessly by Le Pen was, "Who is French?" and the centerpiece of the party platform was the expulsion of immigrants from France.

His percentage of the vote hovered around 10% to 15% from the time he entered the political scene in the early 1970s as president of the National Front party until his daughter, Marine, took over the role. What we see in Le Pen is an odd mix of past and present politics. As Maurice Agulhon puts it: "Le Pen is simultaneously a man of the present and a man of the past. A man of the present in that, as a French nationalist, his xenophobia is anti-immigrant, thus above all, anti-Arab; but (he is) a man of the past in that, counter-revolutionary by tradition, he is equally anti-Semitic."[8] He has played upon the fears of those who feel displaced and/or outnumbered by an influx of "foreigners," who have by now been residents of France for a few generations. Underlying these fears is the belief that France will be contaminated by people from abroad. Richard Bernstein, the author of *Fragile Glory* describes a Le Pen rally at which the "warm-up" singer sang about "le sang de Barbary,"[9] a direct and un-complimentary reference to North Africans living in France.

There are conflicting facets in Le Pen's image of France. On the one hand, Bernstein contends that racial homogeneity has no foundation in French history[10] and that Frenchness must be understood in cultural terms. On the other hand, the National Front's slogan, "France for the French," can be traced back to 1889, when an organization called the National Anti-Semitic League was founded.[11] And Le Pen, unlike his reactionary predecessors, was not part of the system; he remained aberrational or marginal to French politics. He is, indeed, a political leader; he has his following, but he is not about to attempt an overthrow of the Republic like the royalists of the 19th century. Nor is he an agent of death, like the officials of the Vichy regime. By coincidence, on the same day Papon was convicted and sentenced in April 1998, Le Pen was found guilty of assault against a socialist candidate in 1997 and was stripped of his civil rights for two years.

The appeal of the Le Pens has grown steadily over the course of their career in politics. To look at the array of groups who composed their voters is like viewing a replay of politics during the Affair. They are a mix of traditional nationalist Catholics, monarchists, those who are nostalgic for Vichy, and right-wing intellectuals. Their supporters have become more urban and more working class, in contrast to Jean-Marie Le Pen's earlier, more rural support. In examining the Le Pens' rhetoric over the years, one does not find any positive statements of social or economic policy. They repeatedly sound one negative note on domestic policy and that is to rid France of immigrants. The Front is essentially a single-issue party. Its long-term appeal is questionable, if immigrants eventually become integrated in a stable economy. The Le Pens offers nothing to their followers but a return to "traditional" values. A self-described counter-revolutionary, the elder Le Pen's solutions lay in the past and his target was foreigners.

The rise of Jean-Marie Le Pen accelerated in the 1980s. It seemed improbable. In the 1981 elections, Le Pen was so unpopular, he could not collect the 500 signatures required to get on the ballot. He called on his supporters to vote for Jeanne d'Arc instead. The Mitterand socialist government came to power in an easy victory that year, with a progressive social and economic agenda. However, the failure to implement these programs and the subsequent growing unemployment helped raise the profile of Le Pen, who was then able to capture the support of the working class, which had always been allied with leftist parties. Three years later, in 1984, Le Pen won nearly 11 percent of the votes in European parliamentary elections.[12]

Well after the fact, in an analysis for *The Guardian*, Natalie Nougayrede argued, along with the obvious economic and social explanations for Le Pen's success at the polls, that he profited from the inability of the Mitterand government to fulfill their promises for change. Thus, the FN, with its outsider image was able to capitalize on popular discontent. It was not part of the governing establishment and that served as a plus.[13]

In 1995, the FN had gained 15 percent in the first round of the presidential elections and *The New York Times* characterized the FN as "the second party of the French right."[14] The base of support had grown to include workers, although its ideology certainly contained nothing that would appeal to workers economically. There were continuing debates reported in the media over whether the FN was a fascist party or not, with many comparing it to the growing neo-Nazi movement in France.[15]

In 2011, Le Pen's daughter, Marine, wrested leadership of the FN from her father. She wanted to modify the image of the party and broaden its support. Once again, the FN has benefited from the weakness of the mainstream parties. Although Marine has essentially the same platform as her father, the tone is different. She still rouses audiences with her anti-immigration rhetoric, her desire to leave the European Union and the euro, and her nationalistic rhetoric that has been a tune played in France for a very long time.[16] The politics of the Le Pens often seem like a replay of the polarization of public opinion in the Dreyfus Affair.

Le Pen's populist rhetoric and the unemployment figures in France in the 90s certainly account for much of his appeal. Economic insecurity, persisting to this day, is connected to the anger chiefly directed against the Muslim population. Le Pen's stand on immigration even tempted parties on the right to deal with him at one point. The threat of the Far Right upset the conservative moderates to the point that Chirac went on national television in March 1998, after riots orchestrated by Le Pen's followers broke out through the country, to ask conservatives not to have dealings with Le Pen and certainly not to support him in his campaign.[17]

Much of the extremism of Le Pen and his followers has centered in towns in southern France, which have periodically elected Front National mayors. Toulon particularly has been frequently in the limelight. In 1996, the mayor refused to award the book prize at the Toulon Book Fair to Marek Halter, a Jew born in Poland who had fled to France as a child. He revoked the award granted Halter and gave it to Brigitte Bardot, who had written her memoirs and whose husband was a party member. *The New York Times* headline read: "French Book Fair Writhes, Poisoned by Politics."[18] The mayor responded to questions about his anti-Semitism by saying that his action had nothing to do with Halter's being a Jew because, unlike Muslims, "Jews are rarely unemployed." All major publishers boycotted the fair and the Minister of Culture spoke out in support of Halter.

In the city of Orange in the same year, the municipal leaders prohibited the city library from stocking reading material on the French Revolution, World War II, and Arab and African tales for children. With a large North African population in the region, this last restriction was a clear message to immigrants. In angry statements to the press, the mayor railed against multi-culturalism as destructive to France. One city employee described the atmosphere as incriminatory and full of suspicion.

In contemporary France at the end of the 20th century, the question of authentic "Frenchness" was as important an issue as it had been during the Dreyfus years, albeit the focus had shifted from anti-Semitism to anti-foreigner attitudes. Although most countries have had problems accepting immigrants, France would seem to rank among the most xenophobic in concerns over its culture being adulterated. Even among countries that routinely mistreated immigrants as less than full citizens, the cultural threat did not figure so prominently in government policy. In fact, the "melting pot" was accepted sociological theory for a very long period of time in the United States. The problem for France was a rigid definition of nation.

For France, a country that had always resisted pluralism, the choice to go forward as a nation of many distinct groups or as a community of individuals could not be easily resolved. In November 1991, Le Pen, forever a provocateur, proposed detention camps for illegal immigrants, from which they could be deported. He also recommended reducing social benefits and giving French citizens priority in employment. The citizenship issue was another subject on which Le Pen gained approval, when he suggested citizenship pass only through blood ties. In 1993, the French government changed its nationality law so that, instead of becoming French citizens automatically at 18, French born children of immigrants needed to apply for the status between the ages of 14 and 21.

Some interesting conclusions can be drawn about the causes and effects of the Dreyfus Affair and the current situation in France. First, it is evident that numbers have little correlation with race hatred; Jews have never been a sizeable percentage of the French nation. Second, France has not evolved as a country that accepts pluralism or, to use the contemporary phrase, "multi-culturalism." In fact, it holds pluralism in contempt. The preservation of French culture undiluted is the goal. "Multiculturalism would be the end of France," said Pierre Lellouche, a conservative deputy. [19] The U.S. is constantly held up as a bad example of what could happen if cultural and language differences were to be tolerated.

The French are proud of the fact that there are no hyphenated Frenchmen. For the French, multi-culturalism is anti-French, whereas Americans tend to see their culture in transition, adding and dropping certain features as time progresses. On balance, Americans have perceived immigration as a positive addition to their nation, while the French have not. A European Commission report released in 1991 suggests that European nations try to integrate minority populations better, so that they do not become permanently marginalized.

Despite the fact that France is a secular state and a very small percentage of its people are practicing Catholics, other religions are viewed as inimical to French tradition from a cultural perspective. It is interesting that a country with a sharply declining percentage of its population participating in religious marriages, baptisms, and regular church attendance should be so disturbed by the Muslim presence. The religious issue has yet to be addressed calmly.

Le Pen has found a handy target in the observant Muslim population and gathered a lot of support for what has become a major issue in the French school system—the right of Muslim girls to wear headcoverings to school. This is hardly the kind of problem to which a tolerant nation would assign high priority.

Next, the issue of language has proved to be extremely explosive. A reluctance to absorb foreign words into the common vocabulary characterizes the French approach. This can have an adverse effect on business, in a world linked by the Internet. They have absolutely no sense of humor or flexibility about what they consider to be the corruption of their language, which is essential to their culture. The extremes to which the French have gone to find French equivalents for words understood universally in English, even when it makes business difficult, is proof of this.

The legacy of the Dreyfus Affair has been one of conflicting tendencies; there has been a mix of racism and expiation over many decades. Generations after the famous trial, despite strong resistance, the culture has slowly changed, along with the population. There is a serious attempt to look back at history and try to achieve some understanding of this century-old event. This is clearly a benefit in the retelling of the tale and the historic analysis that accompanies it. Many older people were amazed that, in the year 2000, many young French were surprised by an exhibit on collaborationism in France. To parody the French cliché *plus ça change*, the more the French are aware of their past, the more they need to respond by reviewing their history honestly, as the Germans have done.

It took the shock of the Vichy era to motivate the French to come to terms with many longstanding cleavages in their society. The trials of the collaborators, though far removed from the experience of the present generation, have served as an educational tool. In the end, they provide both a lesson and a catharsis. In the nearly 100 years between the first Dreyfus court martial and the trial of Klaus Barbie, the French underwent cataclysmic social, economic, and moral changes: the First World War, the depression of the 1930s, the German Occupation, the Second World War, the difficult post-war recovery, and the ongoing integration of Europe. These events, one might say, were not particular to France, but the depth of the losses—of population and of values—was different from, say the experience of Great Britain or the United States. For, unlike those countries, to paraphrase W. B. Yeats: the center did not hold.

The modern aspect of the Dreyfus trial is worth exploring because we can see, virtually for the first time in a legal proceeding, the effect of a powerful relationship between the media and public opinion. The press became Dreyfus' courtroom and the reading public, his jury. In this sense, the case becomes a model of future political trials in which press coverage plays a dominant role both domestically and globally.

Governments behave differently when the glare of world opinion is focused on them. The citizenry itself begins to feel the pressure of this opinion and its immediate effect on the image of the country. The violent rhetoric of anti-Semitism during the Dreyfus period would be totally unacceptable in today's media, although it lasted unchallenged through the Hitler years. At least in free nations, domestic politics eventually begin to respond to foreign disapproval. In the Dreyfus case, it was the upcoming Paris Exposition of 1900 that was of concern, much as the threat of trade embargos and other economic sanctions influence government policy today.

The Dreyfus Affair proved that political trials extend beyond national borders, once communications are open, and that what other nations think is, indeed, of great importance to the country's image. The linkage between economics and politics, between domestic and foreign policy, is now so recognized, it must be considered in policy making. Had the Dreyfus case occurred today, it is highly unlikely he would have spent five years on Devil's Island in obscurity, without the support of influential groups lobbying hard for his freedom. Think of the mobilization of groups and institutions that would have organized on his behalf a century later. We can turn to the case of Jonathan Pollard, the American Jew accused of spying for Israel, who served time in a U.S. prison until his parole in 2015, for an example of organized political pressure by interest groups on government. A component of all 20th century political trials has been organized group activity. This is very different from the Affair, during which the pressure was global and governmental, modern for its time, but not the result of actions by NGOs and private groups.

Likewise, the story of a rather innocuous army officer framed on a trumped-up charge would have passed into oblivion if the press had not responded to the celebrity of Émile Zola. Zola symbolized the conscience of France and willingly or not, Captain Dreyfus found himself the centerpiece of a battle against injustice. But it took years before Zola's statement set off the reaction that would ultimately save Dreyfus. The price of freedom was intense publicity; the mobilization of public opinion was a very modern concept.

The importance of public opinion and the extent of the press coverage in the Affair were unprecedented. The shift in popular perception from the first court martial to the second at Rennes was palpable. Zola's angry charges of corruption in the military had a profound effect in many sectors. The government began to shift emphasis from unqualified support of the army's position to serious concern about the impact on French trade associated with the opening of the Paris Exposition. The political leadership wanted to show the world it had modernized and was now a major force in world commerce.

Domestic politics was closely tied to the reaction to the Affair in other countries. In the longest entry in its twelve-volume *Jewish Encyclopedia* (Funk and Wagnalls, 1925 edition), the Dreyfus Affair is termed the best-known *cause célèbre* of modern times, since it involved the fate of ministries and even of presidents of the Republic. France, which had once been thought to determine the cultural standards of Western nations, was now experiencing the criticism of these same nations. For the most civilized nation in the world to be held up as an example of modern barbarism was unpalatable medicine to swallow. The French self-image was deeply affected by the strongly negative shift in its global image.

It must be said, before the analogy of France at the turn of the century and France today is stretched too far, that there is an important difference. That difference is crucial and it resides in the institutional framework of the nation. In the time of Dreyfus, powerful institutions—the Church and the Army—were allied against the Republic. When the Vichy government applauded the end of the Third Republic, Philippe Burrin speculates they were unaware they had sacrificed the achievements of the Revolution along with the less savory elements of that upheaval. The values of tradition and order had superseded the values of democracy. Much as they disliked the republican form of government and wished to be rid of it, they may not have realized how much had been lost.

Today, the Le Pens and their supporters have no institutional backing. They remain a force and a reactionary one, but they have no governmental authority to lend legitimacy. They have a point of view; they are heard, but they remain marginal to the politics of France. They do not threaten the existence of the Republic, as their 19th-century predecessors did. As recently as 1994, a book by Renaud Camus (no relation to the great writer/ philosopher) appeared in France and created quite a stir. La campagne de France is an autobiographical narrative by a wealthy Frenchman of aristocratic background. In the course of this narrative, he describes the Jewish threat to French culture, rails against the numbers of Jews in high places, and warns of their pernicious influence on the French economy. The Minister of Culture replied angrily to this anti-Semitic attack and the publisher decided to drop 10 pages from the next edition.

Coincidentally, this occurred exactly 100 years after Dreyfus was accused and court-martialed. Extensive media coverage reinforced the fact that no democratic nation could remain indifferent to fascism in its midst.

So, a lesson has been learned in the legacy of the Affair, over a long period of time. The perceived threat of a republican form of government to established institutions, like the army and the Church, was kept alive from the Revolution, through the Paris Commune uprising, the Dreyfus Affair, and the Vichy government. Yet, that lesson of history has made it clear to the French their political system has survived the challenge of counter-revolutionary movements, the anti-Semitism of Vichy, and the xenophobia and racism of the current leaders of anti-immigrant groups. A terrible price has been paid for this knowledge, but the republic survives.

What if the Dreyfus Affair had never occurred? When we speak of a legacy, the word is used to mean everything in French society that derives from the Affair. It so happened that the case of Captain Dreyfus was the catalyst for forces that were already present. It was this particular miscarriage of justice that highlighted political and social divisions endemic to the French system. Had it not been his trial, issues would have arisen in another arena, around another event. All the forces were present in French society for confrontation. The Church was pitted against the Republic, the role of the Army in the political system demanded clarification, the position of the Jews in society was insecure, the question of nationalism permeated all political debates, and the economy was in trouble. As it was, this one case served to illuminate in the glare of publicity all the tensions and divisions that underlay the social fabric. The man himself was irrelevant, just a tiny boat bobbing on the powerful waves of a potentially dangerous storm.

This trial speaks to us in many ways. Whereas we have seen that, today, a similar case would instantly mobilize established groups and create new ones, this case was initially out of the public view with its *in camera* proceedings. Five years later, the public trial at Rennes generated incredible interest, but the outcome was still unfavorable to Dreyfus, as the military dug in its heels. This was hard to understand for many observers outside French society. For many years, the reputation of the army and the nation were one. The strong connection between the army and national pride was a vital factor in avoiding the obvious truth of Dreyfus' innocence. Institutions change slowly and the Army was not about to reverse itself without a struggle.

Domestic politics in *fin de siècle* France have many parallels in modern France: weak government, anti-Semitism, racism, and the humiliation of the German occupation all serve as reminders of the social and political turmoil of the Dreyfus Affair. Certainly, all states have reactionary movements that want to return to "traditional" values. There is always comfort in returning to the past, for those who fear a changing society. The degree to which they capture the public imagination is what is important; that degree is often determined by an ingrained dissatisfaction with the current regime. Resistant groups are sending a message that should not be ignored. Whether on the right or the left, every democratic regime should pay careful attention to the dissenters.

The assortment of groups with intense opinions that spring up around every well-publicized American political trial were not present in the era of the Dreyfus case. Were there a case with such great political implications today, there would be a host of *amicus curiae* briefs filed to give weight to the arguments of defendants and plaintiffs. Groups would have seized on the case to publicize their points of view. The cause would have been taken up by a huge number of groups, both solicited and unsolicited. Group politics would have been a major force in the outcome. Although society was extremely polarized for and against Dreyfus, for the most part this polarization was not organized.

The responsiveness of the Third Republic leadership to the media was probably due more to concern over the Paris Exposition than for any more serious policy reasons. However, the response, late as it was, was a significant move toward building a democratic model, in which the power structure is relatively open and where more groups are contending for positions of influence in a greater number of spheres.

There are many "publics" for every issue, which can provide a safeguard for the democratic process. France was comparatively slow in developing strong interest groups with access to power. Politicians now realize they need to listen to a broad range of dissenters. A century later, Zola would have been a hero, commanding top fees for speaking engagements, rather than an exile in England. The rules of the game were beginning to change and, with that change, the opportunities for people to speak out and be heard were expanded.

Today's political agenda has a broader scope than that of a century ago. Democracy has evolved over the centuries, to a point where the protection of the individual from governmental abuses has a higher priority than ever before. Our vision has altered; the plight of one man is perceived as an invasion of everyone's rights. The danger to one group is perceived as a danger to all. In this way, the legacy of the Dreyfus Affair endures as a victory for a universal respect of individual rights and a healthy distrust of institutions that attempt to deny those rights. If republican forms of government cannot protect their citizens, then where will they be protected? Think of the vast differences between the courts-martial of Dreyfus and the trials of Pétain, Barbie, and Papon. The uproar surrounding the extradition of Pinochet to Chile serves as another example. That a conservative country like Spain would be demanding extradition and trial for a Latin leader is extraordinary. Justice and democracy are linked. Democracy must be able to recognize and surmount opposition without stifling it. We have learned from the dreadful abuses of the rule of law in the Dreyfus Affair the importance of vigilance in safeguarding democracy through insisting on judicial safeguards by way of procedural standards.

Addendum

WHY THE ENDURING FASCINATION with the Dreyfus Affair? Why are ordinary people and scholars still intrigued by the case? Because no other single event since has had an equivalent impact, or as long-lasting of one, on a nation.

What is unusual about a suspicion of outsiders? Aren't all European nations, and in fact all nations, hostile to outsiders? Yes, but the attitude in France had a nationalistic fervor and intensity that made it qualitatively different. The Le Pens' ongoing battle against outsiders is a good example.

What about Nazism and anti-Semitism in Germany as a comparison? France remains of special interest because, unlike Germany, it was a democracy at the turn of the century. Furthermore, France had a reputation as a country that valued rights and represented a cultural standard other nations might emulate; the Dreyfus Affair challenged this stereotype. France's image and self-confidence suffered badly as a result.

Press coverage was an eye opener as to the power of the media. The unraveling of the coverup, exposed in the press, was more than the army could counter. Secrecy was no longer a viable option for the military. It was clear that one of the oldest and most respected institutions of France was not above the scrutiny of public opinion. Even the Church could not escape the criticism of some of its adherents.

This single case, not so different from other court-martial proceedings, seen in the light of day was a microcosm for the greater problems facing a nation coming of age in industrial society. It provided a window into the culture, history, politics, and psychology of the time. The added dimension of anti-Semitism gave it much more visibility than it would ordinarily have had, but the major sources of conflict—the opposition to republicanism, the fear of economic displacement as urbanization and industrialism moved swiftly ahead, the threat of socialism, the expansion of communication with other nations and other social systems—were truly the heart of the matter. The challenge of counter-revolutionarism was set back—although more as a result of external than internal influences. It was as though the nation had been artfully patched together to hide longstanding fissures. When the plight of one previously unknown army officer ripped off the tape, it revealed what everyone already knew was there, forcing a government and its population to deal with a complexity of problems hitherto ignored.

Afterword

ON A TRIP TO PARIS IN SEPTEMBER 2000, I visited the monument to Dreyfus in a tiny square right next to a grimy Métro stop in the *sixième arrondissement*. It had been dedicated by Jacques Chirac, then mayor of Paris, in October 1994, after much contentious debate over whether and where it should be placed. The statue, home now to many pigeons, looks like a cross between Charles de Gaulle and Don Quixote; the small head on an elongated body gazes out sadly into the street, as though pondering whether this drab urban environment is truly his home.

Later that beautiful, early fall day, my husband and I walked slowly through Montparnasse cemetery, (the resting place for many of France's most famous writers, artists, and composers), in search of the Dreyfus family plot. I was impressed by the large number of Jewish graves. It was not easy to find Dreyfus' among the crowded mass of tombstones. When we did find it, a great sadness enveloped me as I read the names of all those in his family who had perished for France, alongside those, like his granddaughter, who died at Auschwitz. I thought about the unswerving faith the Dreyfuses and so many other Jewish families of the *haute bourgeoisie* had placed in their country, only to be cruelly disappointed. As for Alfred Dreyfus himself? A precise, intensely private man, as his ashes lie under the soil of Montparnasse—the remains of a man whose life had come to symbolize a nation bitterly divided—does his soul rest peacefully, or is he embarrassed and tormented by the somber imprint his experience has left on his country forever?

If part of the legacy of the Dreyfus experience was to remove the blinders from assimilated French Jews, to give them the courage to be Jews in public and identify with others by rallying against anti-Semitism as it resurfaced with Le Pen, it has positive value. Equally, if it has forced French non-Jews to confront the racism in their midst, it provides hope for the future of their country. On the other hand, if there are still those who study the past and refuse to acknowledge the crucial role of anti-Semitism in the Affair, then they haven't learned much from their history and the legacy is meaningless. The reinterpretation of history by succeeding generations is a crucial guide to our present experience.

Above all, we see in the injustice of the Dreyfus Affair the obstacles posed by a homogeneous society to those perceived as outsiders. The different ways in which homogeneous and pluralistic societies deal with dissent is a subject worth studying, for all of us who care about protecting individual rights. We can learn from history and refuse to play old roles, recognizing them for what they are, despite the new casts of characters in new settings. The threat of fascism is always present. We are all placed in danger when governments themselves attack reason and humanism in the name of preserving their culture and values.

When Émile Zola wrote his fiery indictment of the French judicial system and the military, he put a nation on trial. His words magnified a case of treason to become a symbol of injustice. More than 100 years later, France is still on trial, and for many of the same reasons Captain Dreyfus was in his day.

August 15, 2015

Events in 21st century France recall the unfinished business of the Dreyfus Affair in a contemporary context. The theme of chauvinism along with deep divisions over who is authentically French resonate with the issues in French society in the late 19th century, although with a different cast of characters. The impact of the Affair endures.

Plus ça change, plus c'est la même chose is a well-known French saying, particularly relevant to an evaluation of the Dreyfus affair; it leads to consideration of an important question. What has changed since then in France regarding anti-Semitism? At the end of the 19th century, the trial of an "assimilated Jew" convicted of treason in a blatant miscarriage of justice aroused world criticism. All the evidence showed a pervasive anti-Semitism that underlay a web of lies and false statements, resulting in Dreyfus' conviction and sentence to exile. This was accomplished by the military in peacetime after the French defeat in the Franco-Prussian war and was supported by a huge cohort of the French population across many social classes.

On January 13, 2015, after the outcry over two virtually simultaneous horrific incidents in Paris, where journalists of a weekly satirical journal where gunned down by Muslim terrorists and, a few days later, ordinary customers in a kosher butcher shop were murdered in another violent incident, allegedly perpetrated by Jew-hating Muslims, the French government felt compelled to respond. It could no longer ignore the terrorist threats to public safety, when the print and online media overflowed with coverage of and opinion pieces about these atrocities.

Soon after, the French ambassador to the United States, Gerard Araud, came to a Washington synagogue to address an audience, in what was termed " a gathering of solidarity and remembrance with the people of France and its Jewish community."

He spoke to the fears and insecurity of French Jews, who no longer trusted they could live safely in their country. Many had been leaving for Israel and other countries over the past decades, as attacks on Jewish schools and places of worship mounted.

Araud said, "That my French Jewish compatriots could be forced to leave my country, their country, our country, because they are afraid, as my Prime Minister just said, it would be a moral failure if France were not able to protect the Jews of France. France without the Jews of France wouldn't be France…We have been aware for nearly a decade now of the rise of a new type of anti-Semitism."

After reassuring his audience that France was "stepping up" its efforts to protect its Jewish population and moving against hate speech in public life by teaching tolerance in school curricula, the Ambassador asserted that the French would uphold the democratic ideal presently under threat throughout Europe.

Between the wars, French intellectual society teemed with Jewish writers, artists, and musicians. There was also a stellar roster of talent in the world of theater and film. Yet, when it came to the crucial test at the onset of World War II, these people were, for the most part, abandoned to a horrible fate. One such person was Irene Nemirovsky, a convert to Catholicism and a writer who believed, almost to the end, she would survive the roundup of Jews in France, given her connections in high places.

Sadly, this was not to be and she and her husband were hunted down in the south of France, where they had escaped, and sent to concentration camps, where they died. Her last writings, as she realized how little their prestige counted in her possible salvation, are despairing. These handwritten pages were found years later by her surviving daughters in England and published posthumously nearly five decades later, to great acclaim. Like Dreyfus, she had always put her French identity first, although she had Russian Jewish origins. Still, so many years after the sufferings of Alfred Dreyfus, there was little progress with assimilation in France.

What can we conclude, then, about anti-Semitism in French history from Dreyfus' era to the present time? In 2012, when Jewish children were murdered at a school in Lyon, public debate on who was French escalated, as it had before when Le Pen entered politics. For many Muslims, the perception they were considered foreigners no matter how long they had lived in France was alienating. They felt their culture was denigrated or, at best, ignored.

As Ambassador Araud's statements indicate, more than a century after the Dreyfus Affair sharply divided French society, the French have finally been forced to rethink their nationalism and overcome their resistance to pluralism. *On va voir.* We can only wait and see.

Notes on the Text

Introduction: More Than Just a Trial

1. Louis L. Snyder, *The Dreyfus Case* (New Jersey: Rutgers University Press, 1973), p. 284.
2. Ibid., p. 343.

Chapter 1. The Affair: The First Trial

1. E. Austin Farleigh, "A Comparison of British and French Courts-Martial," *Westminster Review 149* (1898), pp. 1–7.
2. *The New York Herald Tribune*, "Intensely Humiliating Punishment of a Convicted Officer," 6 January 1895, p. 5.
3. Jean-Denis Bredin, *The Affair* (New York: George Braziller, Inc., 1986), p. 76.

Chapter 2. The Affair: The Second Trial

1. Jean-Denis Bredin, *The Affair* (New York: George Braziller, Inc., 1986), p. 176.
2. Ibid., p. 198.
3. Barbara Tuchman, *The Proud Tower* (New York: The Macmillan Co., 1966), p. 198.
4. *The New York Times*, 25 February 1898.
5. Robert L. Hoffman, *More Than Just a Trial* (New York: The Free Press, 1980), p. 195.
6. Bredin, *The Affair*, p. 531.

7. Michael Winock, "Les Deux France." *L'Histoire*, No. 173 (1994), p. 65.
8. Jean Doise, "Was French Intelligence Involved?" *L'Histoire*, No. 173 (1994), pp. 28–36.

Chapter 3. Dreyfus: The Disappointing Hero

1. Michael Burns, *Dreyfus: A Family Affair 1789–1945* (London: Chatto and Windus, 1991), pp. 3–25
2. Alfred Dreyfus, *Cinq Années de Ma Vie* (Freeport, NY: Books for Libraries Press), entries for 11 January 1895 (p. 56), 28 February 1896 (p. 202), September 1896 (passim).
3. Burns, *Dreyfus: A Family Affair 1789–1945*, pp. 392–393.
4. Jean-Denis Bredin, *The Affair* (New York: George Braziller, 1983), p. 500.

Chapter 4. The Historical Context

1. Eric Hobsbawm, *The Age of Empire 1875-1914* (New York: Vintage Books, 1989), p. 96.
2. Albert Guerard, *France: A Modern History* (Ann Arbor: The University of Michigan Press, 1954), p. 245.
3. Ibid., p. 267.
4. Stephen Wilson, "The Antisemitic Riots of 1898 in France," *The Historical Journal* (XVI No. 4, December 1973), pp. 789–806.
5. Maurice Agulhon, *The French Republic 1879–1992* (Oxford: Blackwell, 1993), p. 56.
6. Ernst Pavel, *The Labyrinth of Exile: A Life of Theodor Herzl* (New York: Farrar, Straus & Giroux, 1989), p. 162.

7. Jean-Denis Bredin, *The Affair* (New York: George Braziller, 1983), p. 288.

8. Félix Aucaigne, "The Dreyfus Case and the Anti-Semitic Outbreak in France," *Harper's Weekly*, Vol. 42, No. 139 (1898), passim.

9. Agulhon, *The French Republic 1879–1992*, p. 111.

10. Ibid., p. 70.

11. Ibid., p. 90.

12. Gordon Wright, *France in Modern Time*, 3rd edition (New York and London: W. W. Norton and Company, 1981), p. 259.

13. *The New York Times*, 17 October 1906, 6:4.

14. Nicolas Halasz, *Captain Dreyfus: The Story of Mass Hysteria* (New York: Simon & Schuster, 1955), p.125.

Chapter 5. The Pitched Battle: Dreyfusards versus Anti-Dreyfusards

1. J. Hampden Jackson, *Jean Jaures, His Life and Work* (New York: W. W. Norton and Co., 1943), p. 77.

2. Pierre Birnbaum, "L' Armée française était-elle antsémite?" Edition: "L' Affaire Dreyfus: Vérités et Mensonges," *L'Histoire*, 17 January 1994, p. 67.

3. Eric Fassin, "Play It Again, Sartre?" *French Politics and Society 16:1* (Winter 1998), pp. 25–58.

Chapter 6. Anti-Semitism in Europe in the 19th Century

1. William Shirer, *The Collapse of the Third Republic* (New York: Simon and Schuster, 1969), p. 21.

2. Alan Riding. "A Close-Up of Artists Who Made Paris Sizzle," *The New York Times*, 11 January 2001, p. B1.

3. Jean-Denis Bredin, *The Affair* (New York: George Braziller, 1983), p. 23.

4. Preface to *Cinq Années de Ma Vie* (Paris: Fasquelle, 1962), p. 13.

5. Bernard Lazare, *L'antisemitisme: Son histoire et ses causes*, Paris, 1894, p. 227, quote in Bredin, *The Affair*, p. 25.

6. Robert Hoffman, *More Than a Trial* (New York: The Free Press, 1980), p. 70.

7. Alex Bein, translated by Maurice Samuel, *Herzl: A Biography* (Vienna: Fiba Verlag, 1935), passim.

8. Hoffman, *More Than a Trial*, p. 69.

9. Lazare, quote in Bredin, *The Affair*, p. 29.

10. Adolphe Willette, 1889 election poster, public domain, via Wikimedia Commons.

11. Joseph Reinach, *L'Histoire Sommaire de l'Affaire Dreyfus* (Paris: Fasquelle, 1924), passim.

12. Lazare, quote in Bredin, p. 30.

13. Nancy Fitch, "Mass Culture, Mass Parlimentary Politics and Modern Anti-Semitism," *The American Historical Review* 97 (1992), pp. 55–95.

14. Leon Blum, *Souvenirs sur l'Affaire Dreyfus* (Paris: Gallimard, 1982), p.43.

15. Shirer, *The Collapse of the Third Republic*, p. 60.

16. Hoffman, p. 69.

17. Ron Rosenbaum. *Explaining Hitler* (New York: Random House, 1998), p. 302.

18. Hoffman, p. 71.

19. Bredin, *The Affair*, p. 289.

20. H.G. de Blowitz, "The French Press and the Dreyfus Case," *The North American Review*, Vol. 169, No. 515 (October, 1899), p. 592.

21. Maurice Barrès, *Scènes et Doctrines du nationalisme* (Paris: Félix Guven, 1902), p. 152.

22. Edward R. Tannenbaum, *The Action Française* (New York and London: John Wiley and Sons, Inc., 1962), p. 93.

23. Ibid., p. 136.

24. Ibid., p. 144.

25. Ibid., p. 264.

26. Hoffman, p. 157.

Chapter 7. Media in the Dreyfus Affair: The Force of Public Opinion

1. "Intensely Humiliating Punishment of a Convicted Officer," *The New York Times*, 6 January 1895, 5:1.

2. *The New York Herald Tribune*, 6 January 1895, 9:1.

3. Émile Zola, "J'Accuse...! Lettre au Président de la République," Zola's letter was first published on the front page of *L'Aurore* on 13 January 1898 in France and was subsequently republished in countless newspapers worldwide.

4. Jean-Denis Bredin, *The Affair* (New York: George Braziller, 1983), p. 250.

5. Funeral oration delivered by Anatole France, 5 October 1902, www.dreyfus.culture.fr/en.

6. David L. Lewis, *Prisoners of Honor* (New York: Wm. Morrow and Co., Inc., 1973), p. 299.

7. Bredin, *The Affair*, p. 346.

8. Ibid., p. 353.

9. *The New York Times*, "Demange Pleads for Dreyfus," editorial, 9 September 1899, p. 2.

10. Louis L. Snyder, *The Dreyfus Case* (New Jersey: Rutgers University Press, 1973), p. 332.

11. Ibid., p. 301.

12. *The New York Herald Tribune*, "The Day in France," editorial, 5 August 1899.

13. Nancy Fitch, "Mass Culture, Mass Parlimentary Politics, and Modern Anti-Semitism: The Dreyfus Affair in Rural France," *American Historical Review*, Vol. 97 (1992), passim.

14. Eric Cahm, "L'Affaire Dreyfus dans la presse quotidienne allemande 1897–1899," Michel Denis, Michel Lagrée, and Jean-Yves Veillard, editors, *L'Affaire Dreyfus et l'opinion publique en France et à l'etranger*, (Rennes: Presses universitaires de Rennes, 1995), p. 222.

15. Roderick Kedward, *The Dreyfus Affair* (London: Longmans, 1963), p. 11.

16. G.W. Steevens, "France as Affected by the Dreyfus Case," *Harper's*, October 1889, p. 792.

17. *The Nation*, No. 67, 18 August 1898, p. 126.

18. Frederick W. Whitridge, "Zola, Dreyfus, and the French Republic," *Political Science Quarterly*, Vol. 13, No. 2, 1898, pp. 259–272.

19. *The Spectator*, 30 September 1899, p. 436.

20. *The Westminster Review*, "The Dreyfus Case and the Future of France," Vol. 152 No. 4, October 1889, pp. 357–68.

21. *The New York Times*, "Dreyfus in Switzerland: Living Quietly in Geneva—Grateful to America and *The Times*," 28 August 1906, 6:7.

22. Cahm, *L'Affaire Dreyfus et l'opinion publique en France et à l'etranger*, p. 293.

23. Nelly Wilson, "Paroles et silence: reflexions sur le rôle joue par la presse britannique dans l'affaire Dreyfus," *L'Affaire Dreyfus et l'opinion publique en France et à l'etranger*, pp. 291–305.

24. Andre Kaspi, "La France Au Ban des Nations," *L'Histoire*, No. 173 (1994), p. 99.

25. Quote in John Cornwell, *Hitler's Pope* (Viking: New York, 1999), p. 45.

26. Jean-Dominique Durand, "Le Saint-siege et l'affaire Dreyfus," *L'Affaire Dreyfus et l'opinion publique en France et à l'etranger*, pp. 127-147.

27. Steevens, *Harper's*, pp. 797–798.

28. Daniel Halévy, "Apologie pour notre passé," *Luttes et problèmes*, pp. 29-30, 42-45, 47.

Chapter 8. The Vichy Era

1. Ernest Lavisse, quoted in Jean-Denis Bredin, *The Affair* (New York: George Braziller, 1983), p. 531.

2. Robert Hoffman, *More Than a Trial* (New York: The Free Press, 1980), p. 34.

3. Michael Burns, *Dreyfus: A Family Affair 1789-1945* (London: Chatto and Windus, 1991), p. 361.

4. Ibid., p. 461.

5. Michael R. Marrus and Robert O. Paxton, *Vichy France and the Jews* (New York: Basic Books, Inc., 1981), p. 53.

6. Quote from an interview with a son of a Vichy Cabinet Minister by Adam Nossiter in *The Algeria Hotel* (New York and Boston: Houghton Mifflin Company, 2001), p. 175.

7. Burns, *Dreyfus: A Family Affair 1789-1945*, p. 466.

8. Ibid., p. 468.

9. Milton Dank, *The French Against the French* (Philadelphia and New York: J.P. Lippincott, 1974), p. 230.

10. Ibid., pp. 225–230.

11. Robert O. Paxton, *Vichy France: Old Guard and New Order, 1940–1944* (New York: Alfred A. Knopf, 1972), p. 143.

12. Marrus and Paxton, *Vichy France and the Jews*, p. 359.

13. Nossiter, *The Algeria Hotel*, p.182.

14. Philippe Burrin, *France Under the Germans* (New York: The New Press, 1996), p. 17.

15. Hannah Arendt, *Eichmann in Jerusalem: A Report on the Banality of Evil* (New York: Viking Press, 1963), passim.

16. Dank, *The French Against the French*, p. 85.

17. Ibid., p. 90.

18. Kathleen McCaffrey, "Breaking the Silence," *Commonweal* (July 17, 1987), pp. 418–20.

19. Robert O. Paxton, *Vichy France Old Guard and New Guard 1940–1944* (New York: Alfred A. Knopf, 1972), p. 66.

20. George Steiner, quoted in Ron Rosenbaum, *Explaining Hitler* (New York: Random House, 1998), p. 302.

21. Christophe de Chenay, "L'ancien camp de Drancy devient monument historique," *Le Monde*, 30 May 2001, p. 13.

22. Ralph Blumenthal, "Holocaust Survivors Sue French Railroad," *The New York Times*, 13 June 2001, p. 12.

23. Marrus and Paxton, p. 348.

24. John Cornwell, *Hitler's Pope* (Viking: New York, 1999), p. 288.

25. Marrus and Paxton, p. 272.

26. Ibid., pp. 365–367.

27. Ibid., p. 359.

28. David L. Lewis, *Prisoners of Honor* (New York: Wm. Morrow and Co., Inc., 1973), p. 325.

29. J. Hampden Jackson, *Jean Jaurès* (New York: W.W. Norton and Co., Inc., 1943), p. 83.

Chapter 9. The Aftermath of the Affair: Unfinished Business

1. Jane Kramer, "Letter from Europe," *The New Yorker*, 12 October, 1987, pp. 130–144.

2. Ibid., p. 136.

3. *The New York Times*, 11 September 2000, p. A6.

4. Jane Kramer, *The New Yorker*, p. 132–134.

5. Ibid., p. 141.

6. Ibid., p. 144.

7. Richard Bernstein, this slogan reported as traceable to 1889 when Jacques de Biez founded the Anti-Semitic League in France, *Fragile Glory* (New York: Alfred A. Knopf, 1990), pp. 104 & 148.

8. Maurice Agulhon, *The French Republic 1879–1992*, Oxford: Blackwell (1992), p. 467.

9. Bernstein, *Fragile Glory*, p. 104.

10. Ibid., p. 113.

11. Ibid., p. 152.

12. Katherine Dwyer, "France's New Nazis: The Resistible Rise of Jean-Marie Le Pen," *International Socialist Review*, online edition, Issue 2, Fall 1997, http://www.isreview.org/issues/02/LePen.shtml.

13. Natalie Nougayrède, "France's cowardly elite is to blame for the rise of Marine Le Pen," *The Guardian*, online edition, 7 December 2015, http://www.theguardian.com/commentisfree/2015/dec/07/marine-le-pen-front-national-france-cowardly-elite.

14. Roger Cohen, "French Far Right May Back the Left in Vote To-morrow," *The New York Times*, archived online, 31 May 1997, http://www.nytimes.com/1997/05/31/world/french-far-right-may-back-the-left-in-vote-tomorrow.html.

15. Dwyer, *International Socialist Review*, online edition.

16. David Chazan, "Marine Le Pen revives plan to rename Front National," *The Telegraph*, 19 December 2015, http://www.telegraph.co.uk/news/worldnews/europe/france/12059738/Marine-Le-Pen-revives-plan-to-rename-Front-National.html.

17. *The Economist*, "On the March," 29 March 2014, http://www.economist.com/news/leaders/21599773-marine-le-pens-success-should-serve-warning-political-elite-france-and-across.html.

18. Roger Cohen, "French Book Fair Writhes, Poisoned by Politics," *The New York Times*, 22 November 1996, http://www.nytimes.com/1996/11/22/world/french-book-fair-writhes-poisoned-by-politics.html.

19. *World Press Review*, January 1998, pp. 8–9.

Bibliography

Books

Agulhon, Maurice. *The French Republic 1879-1992*. Oxford: Blackwell, 1993.

Bernstein, Richard. *Fragile Glory*. New York: Alfred A. Knopf, 1990.

Bredin, Jean-Denis. *The Affair: The Case of Alfred Dreyfus*. New York: George Braziller, 1983.

Burns, Michael. *Dreyfus: A Family Affair 1789-1945*. London: Chatto and Windus, 1991.

Burrin, Philippe. *France Under the Germans*. Translated by Janet Lloyd. New York: The New Press, 1996.

Carroll, James. *Constantine's Sword*. Houghton Mifflin: Boston and New York, 2001.

Cornwell, John. *Hitler's Pope*. Viking: New York, 1999.

Dank, Milton. *The French Against the French*. J.B. Lippincott: Philadelphia and New York, 1974.

Denis, Michel; Michel Lagree; and Jean-Yves Veillard, eds. *L'Affaire Dreyfus et l'opinion publique en France et a l'étranger* (includes articles by

Cahm, Eric; Durand, Jean-Dominique; Wilson, Nelly). Rennes: Presses universitaires de Rennes, 1995.

Dreyfus, Alfred. *Cinq annees de ma vie.* translated by James Mortimer. Books for Libraries Press: Freeport: New York, 1971.

Fenby, Jonathan. *France on the Brink.* Arcade Publishing: New York, 1999.

Feldman, Egal. *The Dreyfus Affair and the American Conscience 1895–1906.* Detroit: Wayne State University Press, 1981.

Halasz, Nicholas. *Captain Dreyfus: The Story of a Mass Hysteria.* New York: Simon and Schuster, 1955.

Hobsbawm, Eric. *The Age of Empire 1875–1914.* New York: Vintage Books, 1989.

Hoffman, Robert L. *More Than a Trial.* New York: The Free Press, 1980.

Hoffman, Stanley. *Decline or Renewal? France Since the 1930s.* New York: Viking, 1974.

IIyman, Paula. *From Dreyfus to Vichy.* New York: Columbia University Press, 1979.

Jackson, J. Hampden. *Jean Jaures: His Life and Work.* New York: W.W. Norton, 1943.

Kedward, Roderick. *The Dreyfus Affair.* London: Longmans, 1963.

Lewis, David L. *Prisoners of Honor.* New York: Wm. Morrow and Co., Inc., 1973.

Lottman, Herbert R. *The French Rothschilds: The Great Banking Dynasty Through Two Turbulent Centuries.* New York: Crown, 1995.

Marrus, Michael R. and Robert O. Paxton. *Vichy France and the Jews.* New York: Basic Books, Inc., 1981.

Nossiter, Adam. *The Algeria Hotel.* Boston and New York: Houghton Mifflin Company, 2001.

Pavel, Ernst. *The Labyrinth of Exile: A Life of Theodor Herzl.* New York: Farrar, Straus & Giroux, 1989.

Paxton, Robert O. *Vichy France: Old Guard and New Order, 1940-1944.* New York: Alfred A. Knopf, 1972.

Reinach, Theodore. *Histoire sommaire de l'affaire Dreyfus.* Paris: Ligue des Droits de L'Homme, 1924.

Rosenbaum, Ron. *Explaining Hitler.* New York: Random House, 1998.

Rousso, Henry. *The Vichy Syndrome.* Cambridge: Harvard University Press, 1991.

Schama, Simon. *Two Rothschilds and the Land of Israel.* New York: Alfred A. Knopf, 1978.

Schom, Alam. *Émile Zola: A Biography*. New York: Henry Holt and Co., Inc., 1987.

Shirer, William. *The Collapse of the Third Republic*. New York: Simon and Schuster, 1969.

Snyder, Louis L. *The Dreyfus Case*. New Brunswick, NJ: Rutgers University Press, 1973.

Tannenbaum, Edward R. *The Action Française*. New York and London: John Wiley & Sons, Inc., 1962.

Thomson, David. *Democracy in France Since 1870*. London: Oxford University Press, 1969.

Tifft, Susan E. and Alex S. Jones. *The Trust*. Boston, New York and London: Little, Brown and Company, 1999.

Tuchman, Barbara W. *The Proud Tower*. New York: The Macmillan Company, 1966.

Vidal-Naquet, Pierre. *The Jews*. Translated and edited by David Ames Curtis. New York: Columbia University Press, 1996.

Watson, David Robin. *Georges Clemenceau, A Political Biography*. New York: David McKay Company, Inc., 1974.

Weber, Eugen. *France Fin de Siècle*. Cambridge, Mass. and London: Belknap Press of Harvard University Press, 1986.

Wright, Gordon. *France in Modern Times (Third Edition)*. New York and London: W.W. Norton and Company, 1981.

Periodicals

Aucaigne, Felix. "The Dreyfus Case and the Anti-Semitic Outbreak in France." *Harper's Weekly*, Vol.42 (5 February 1898): 139.

Burns, Michael. Review by Stephen Wilson. "Ideology and Experience: Anti-Semitism in France at the Time of the Dreyfus Affair." *Social History*, (9 May 1984): 258.

de Blowitz, H.G. "The French Press and the Dreyfus Case." *North American Review* (October 1899): 577–592.

Doise, Jean. "Et si les services secrets Français etaient responsables de l'affaire?" *L'Histoire*, No. 173 (January 1994): 28–34.

Farleigh, E. Austin. "A Comparison of British and French Courts-Martial." *Westminister Review*, Vol. 149 (January 1898): 1–7.

Fassin, Eric. "Play It Again, Sartre?" *French Politics and Society* Vol. 16, No. 1 (Winter 1998): 23–38.

Fitch, Nancy. "Mass Culture, Mass Parliamentary Politics and Modern Anti-Semitism: The Dreyfus Affair in Rural France." *American Historical Review*, Vol. 97 (1992): 55–95.

Gopnik, Adam. "Papon's Paper Trial." *The New Yorker*, Vol. 74, No. 10 (1998): 86–95.

July, Serge. "Tearing Away 50 Years of Lies." Liberation in *World Press Review*, Vol. 45, No. 7 (January 1998).

Kaspi, Andre. "La France au Ban des Nations." *L'Histoire*, No. 173, (January 1994): 96–102.

Kramer, Jane. "Letter from Europe." *The New Yorker* (12 October 1987): 130–144.

L'Express. Interview with Simone Weil in *World Press Review*, Vol. 45, No. 7 (January 1998).

Lichfield, John. "Sins of the Past on Trial." *World Press Review*, Vol. 45, No. 7 (January 1998): 6–7.

Lyon, Ernest Neal. "A Poem to Dreyfus." *Harper's Weekly* (23 September 1899).

McCaffrey, Kathleen. "Breaking the Silence." *Commonweal*, Vol. 114 (17 July 1987): 418–420.

Moisi, Dominique. "The Trouble with France." *Foreign Affairs*. Vol. 77, No. 3 (May/June 1998): 94.

The Nation, editorial, Vol. 67 (18 August 1898): 126.

Ophuls, Marcel. "Klaus Barbie's Circus of Evil." *The Nation*, Vol. 244 (27 June 1998): 884–887.

Ory, Pascal. "Le Tumulte de Rennes." *L'Histoire*, No. 173 (January 1994): 48–52.

Paxton, Robert O. "The Trial of Maurice Papon." *The New York Review of Books*, Vol. 46, No. 21 (1999): p. 32.

Singer, Daniel. "France's Rival Führers." *The Nation*, Vol. 268, No. 6 (15 February 1999): 6–7.

Spectator, The. "The Political Consequences of the Dreyfus Case." (30 September 1899): 435–36.

Steevens, G. W. "France as Affected by the Dreyfus Case." *Harper's Weekly*, Vol. 99 (October 1899): 792–798.

Vaisse, Maurice et Jean-Francois Boulanger. "La Conspiration des Militaires." *L'Histoire*, No. 173 (January 1994): 12–22.

Viner, Richard. "Papon in Perspective." *History Today*, Vol. 48 (July 1998): 6–8.

Warner, Judith. "Guilty But Not Very." *Newsweek*, Vol. 31, No. 15 (13 April 1998): 41.

Weber, Eugen. "Nationalism and the Politics of Resentment." *The American Scholar*, Vol. 63 (Summer 1994): 421–428.

Wernick, Robert. "A Shifty-Eyed Spy Who Was Likely the Nastiest Man Ever." *Smithsonian*, Vol. 20, No. 5 (August 1989).

Whitridge, Frederick W. "Dreyfus and the French Republic." *Political Science Quarterly*, Vol. 13 (June 1898): 259–272.

Wolf, Lucien. "Anti-Semitism and the Dreyfus Case." *The Fortnightly Review* (January 1898): 135–146.

Online Materials

Aurelie, B. and M. Caroline. "Le Front National: Histoire d'un parti d'extreme droite." Internet. 1 December 2000. http://www.ac-clermont.fr/mauriac/ed-d-fro.htm.

Chazan, David. "Marine Le Pen revives plan to rename Front National." *The Telegraph*. Internet. 19 December 2015. http://www.telegraph.co.uk/news/worldnews/europe/france/12059738/Marine-Le-Pen-revives-plan-to-rename-Front-National.html.

Dwyer, Katherine. "France's New Nazis: The Resistible Rise of Jean-Marie Le Pen." *International Socialist Review*. Internet. Issue 2. Fall 1997. http://www.isreview.org/issues/02/LePen.shtml.

The Economist. "On the March." 29 March 2014. http://www.economist.com/news/leaders/21599773-marine-le-pens-success-should-serve-warning-political-elite-france-and-across.

Nougayrède, Natalie. "France's cowardly elite is to blame for the rise of Marine Le Pen." *The Guardian*. Internet. 7 December 2015. http://www. theguardian.com/commentisfree/2015/dec/07/marine-le-pen-front-national-france-cowardly-elite.

Willete, Adolphe. "1889 French election poster for antisemitic candidate Adolphe Willette." Internet. 1889. https://commons.wikimedia.org/ wiki/File%3A1889_French_election_poster_for_antisemitic_candidate_ Adolphe_Willette.jpg.

Made in the USA
Middletown, DE
09 December 2016